SOCIAL MEDIA
RULES OF ENGAGEMENT

SOCIAL MEDIA
RULES OF ENGAGEMENT

WHY YOUR ONLINE NARRATIVE IS
THE BEST WEAPON DURING A CRISIS

NICOLE MATEJIC

WILEY

First published in 2015 by John Wiley & Sons Australia, Ltd
42 McDougall St, Milton Qld 4064
Office also in Melbourne

Typeset in 11/13.5 pt Myriad Pro by Aptara, India

© Invocantis Pty Ltd 2015

The moral rights of the author have been asserted

National Library of Australia Cataloguing-in-Publication data:

Title:	Social Media Rules of Engagement: why your online narrative is the best weapon during a crisis / Nicole Matejic.
ISBN:	9780730322252 (pbk.)
	9780730322269 (ebook)
Notes:	Includes index.
Subjects:	Internet in public relations.
	Social media — Planning.
	Crisis management — Case studies.
Dewey Number:	659.202854678

Cover design: Wiley

Cover images: Bomb icon: ©Alex Belomlinsky/iStockphoto.com;
Background texture: © aleksandarvelasevic/iStockphoto.com

Printed in Singapore by C.O.S. Printers Pte Ltd

10 9 8 7 6 5 4 3 2 1

Disclaimer

This book is dedicated to my village of support.*

---

* http://nicolematejic.com/my-village-of-support/

Contents

About the author

An online trailblazer with a mission, Nicole Matejic is an internationally recognised military information operations adviser and social media crisis communicator.

From the cyber-trenches fighting terrorism on the social media battlefield to the boardrooms of Australian government departments, Parliament House and blue-chip multinationals, Nicole is known for her proactive, innovative and no-BS approach to managing crises and complex issues.

Wearing two hats, Nicole is:

- the co-founder and CEO of global military think tank Info Ops HQ, delivering training to military forces in information operations in the social media battlespace. A regular lecturer to NATO, Nicole speaks around the world on the topics of social media jihad and social media warfare. Visit www.infoopshq.com

- also known as The #SocialFirefighter®. Nicole founded and is CEO of the Australian social media crisis communications consultancy Social Media Monster, providing specialist crisis communications services, training, strategy and preparedness simulations to the public and private sectors. Visit www.socialmediamonster.com.au

Want to find out more about Nicole?

Follow on Twitter:	www.twitter.com/nicolematejic
Follow on Instagram:	www.instagram.com/nicolematejic
Connect on LinkedIn:	www.linkedin.com/in/nicolematejic
Like her Facebook page:	www.facebook.com/thenicolematejic
Subscribe to her YouTube channel:	https://www.youtube.com/channel/ UCQSLuwl3IOuHDPIuavIXnFw
Visit her website:	www.nicolematejic.com

Author note

Before you immerse yourself in this book, you should know it's much more than just ink, paper and pixels. It's a conversation, a #CrisisComms and Info Ops #IOinAction community.

With the purchase of this book you receive access to the Social Media Rules of Engagement online resource portal 'SMROE-HQ', which will keep you updated with real-life and real-time examples of organisational crisis that relate to each chapter in my book.

You can read it the old-fashioned way, from cover to cover, or you can just dive straight into the chapters you find most relevant. Whichever way you read *Social Media Rules of Engagement*, you can choose your own learning adventure by interacting with me directly during your journey: tweet[1] me, leave me a comment[2] or join my book club on BookShout.

I look forward to talking #CrisisComms and #IOinAction with you soon!

Nicole

---

1. https://twitter.com/nicolematejic
2. https://www.facebook.com/thenicolematejic

NATO needs social media more than social media needs NATO … It is critical that you are out in front managing your message so that you do it yourself; if you don't, someone will do it for you and not always with the best intentions.

Franky Saegerman
Head of NATO Social Media

Preface

2008. Canberra. I was working in intelligence.

As an analyst, you have two choices:

1 Follow the status quo — the tried and tested methodology of finding your targets.

2 Forge a new path.

I've never been particularly good at playing follow-the-leader. My brain just isn't wired with the collective groupthink mentality required for life in a hive, so I went off on what was considered at the time a fairly left-field tangent.

Having convinced my then boss to let me loose on the internet (read: humour me for a time), I set up a fake Facebook profile, loaded up a series of Google Alerts and the hunt was on.

What I found was a treasure trove of information about persons of interest. Forget about digital breadcrumbs; these people were tossing whole loaves of bread behind them as they went about their daily lives. It was a photo-frenzied orgy of people, places, contact information and connections.

Social media was in its early sociological renaissance. People were so enamoured with just the thought of being part of this exciting new phenomenon that they had very few online inhibitions.

I remember this moment vividly. From an intelligence analyst's perspective, I'd hit the data jackpot! Forget about months of legwork to track down the name of a single person of interest's associate. I just had to search their Facebook friends list, cross-reference that with information from classified sources and verify my data.

In a very short time, riding on the high of some early successes, I began teaching a few others in my unit the tools of my newly forged trade. Those early successes were significant, not only because they proved that a seismic shift in open source intelligence (OSINT, or publically available information) gathering had occurred from a theoretical standpoint, but also because *it worked*.

We were finding persons and activities of interest that in all likelihood would have taken a fair amount of traditional tradecraft to discover. Those in the game know only too well that gathering intelligence successfully is an uneasy marriage of exceptional behind-the-scenes groundwork and covert or overt in-situ intervention. All things being equal, the groundwork sets up those conducting the intervention for success — but sometimes one side or the other (or factors outside your control) can let the team down and the whole operation is a bust.

Social media and Google Alerts irrevocably changed the game. The deck was now stacked in the house's favour — and incredibly, it was the persons of interest doing the stacking!

After a particularly timely left-field discovery on a blog from Europe, I found myself running training sessions for a range of agencies. It was the start of my enduring love affair with social media and online data within a law enforcement, and later military, information operations environment.

It wasn't until some five years later that The #SocialFirefighter® was born out of my work in a seemingly endless cycle of crisis- and issues-management roles. I often joked with my colleagues that I should have been a firefighter — because all I seemed to do was extinguish other people's media, public affairs and social media fires. As I began working more and more in the social and digital space, the moniker evolved and I decided to adopt it as a brand.

In a way, I've come full circle. From my beginnings in the media as a freelance photojournalist to digital sales and marketing — falling into surveillance work and spending nearly six years in operational law enforcement roles, rounded out with a further four years of corporate public sector adventures — I now find myself back where I started: in front of my Mac, looking for the next story, a new angle, a different approach.

What then fell under the OSINT umbrella now has its own identity — social engineering. The digital landscape has evolved beyond anything I could have dreamed up back in 2008, and with that evolution has come a range of new risks and challenges.

One of my earliest observations in using social media as an intelligence source was the inherent trust each individual places in those with whom they network. The company you keep online literally guards your privacy. Any one of your connections could be an avenue for infiltration or exploitation.

Social media's dynamically responsive nature presents both opportunities and threats. As a tool of modern communication and marketing, it has a starring role in the way the global population consumes information. As an influence activity conduit, it is highly effective and can be strategically targeted, monetised and measured.

On the flipside, social media can be a very risky, unpredictable proposition. Run in isolation of your broader business objectives, or by staff ill-equipped to effectively communicate or manage social communities and the nuances that arise, it can be a complete disaster. Whether you are online and socially active, offline and socially silent or somewhere in between is irrelevant to the conversations and transactions occurring in the social sphere.

Who should read this book

If you work in the private or public sector, in military strategic communications, information operations, public affairs, crisis- and issues-management, or corporate affairs, this book will give you some insight into how to manage your social media presence to avoid it managing you.

My anecdotes may have a law enforcement or military flavour, but the topics explored are just as relevant to the boardroom, broader government, not-for-profits and the private sector as they are to the battlefield.

One of the most common questions I'm asked once people find out I'm a professional crisis communicator is what 'big #PRFails' have I worked on. I understand their curiosity but it's a question I can't really answer, because I'm paid to keep secrets. My clients, my past and present employers, and those who will hire me in the future trust me with their secrets.

What I can tell you is that I've worked on issues and crises you've certainly read about in the pages of newspapers here in Australia, and some of those stories were republished around the world. You've seen them on the nightly news. Some, of course, have been social media fodder.

I am the silent voice behind the overwhelmed CEO's face. I have been a speechwriter for federal ministers. I was the fly-by-the-tweet-of-your-pants analyst trawling hashtags and social chatter to ensure you are safe and criminals are brought to justice.

In this book I share with you the stories (or fragments thereof) that won't get me arrested.

For case studies and current examples, visit SMROE-HQ at www.socialmediarulesofengagement.com.

PART I

RULES OF ENGAGEMENT

Social media crisis communications:
a seismic shift in the risk profile

I was a child of the digital revolution. By the time I started my undergraduate degree in 1998, the bleeps and pings that were dial-up internet had already started to change the way people communicated.

Email had to be checked 'at least a few times a week'; web pages were a revelation of slow-loading information; and the move to digital photography was an incredible disruption to how we had traditionally captured moments in time.

By the time I was working as a surveillance operative just a few years later, the legal minefield of the digital revolution saw governments racing to update their legislation in an effort to keep up with digital consumerism (and hedonism) as digital devices were used for an ever wider range of legal and, of course, illicit purposes.

The other race being run in the digital revolution was the race to break news. With the print news media's first forays into online news, photojournalists became pseudo-reporters and websites became adjunct news services.

I often refer to the early noughties as a time when the global population developed their information-crack addiction. We just couldn't get enough. Technology-possessed people were like disciples waiting for the Second Coming. Our new temple was the internet and within it we were chasing the digital messiah like junkies chasing the dragon.

From the first digital testament and revelations of Alta Vista and Netscape then Yahoo, Google and Bing, to the second digital testament and revelations of MySpace, Facebook, Twitter, Flickr, Tumblr, Instagram, LinkedIn … search and social networking have become our modern-day prophets, heralding in a seismic change in the way we communicate, connect and share.

Imagine the relative simplicity of being a crisis communicator before the early noughties, when print news ran to editorial deadlines that could span days and photographs took hours to be developed and printed. If the evening news wanted a story they had to send out a news truck with a reporter and camera crew, and getting hold of the videotape after the story had aired was another challenge entirely.

After the newspapers had run their stories of scandal they became tomorrow's fish and chip paper. Radio, feeding off the print news media, was perhaps the biggest antagonist in a crisis because of their inherently short production lead times. In making stories 'newsworthy' they directly influenced how long a crisis could be sustained, and talkback radio gave a voice to the unheard.

Can you imagine the luxury of such an uncomplicated, 9 to 5 professional life?

No blinking Blackberry or iPhone chimes to monitor. No tweets, posts or surprise YouTube embarrassments. No bloggers, citizen journalists or armchair generals to offer their opinions.

While the digital revolution changed the way we communicate, the times they keep on a-changing. The what-next mentality now feeds the consumer technology product cycle from one device to its upgrade and beyond. Can you think of a single aspect of your life that isn't touched by digital or social media in some way?

In the race for the next news fix to feed a global population of information addicts, the digital revolution has not come without its challenges for communicators.

Our audiences are now hungrier for information that ever before.

> They want to digest it quickly, concisely and in real time.
>
> Their bullshit meter is well developed.
>
> They have a *voice*.
>
> They have *influence*.
>
> *They don't need the news media to generate news.*

Crises have gone from largely contained events to broadly uncontainable disasters that might have been preventable but are now impossible to erase.

This seismic shift in the organisational risk profile didn't occur as a by-product of the digital revolution; it occurred because organisations failed to keep pace with the rate of digital consumerism. While children of the revolution were all worshipping at the temple of the internet, organisations were still conducting business like it was 1979.

As organisations waited (some are still waiting) for the social media 'fad' to pass, they failed to innovate. They resisted changes to the way they *needed* to communicate. They lost sight of the moving target that was their audience: their customers, their staff and their shareholders.

Strategic communications foresight was traded in for crisis communications hindsight; and in the rush to recover lost communications ground, they found their savvy digital competitors and adversaries had already lapped them in the race for online influence.

Cue the modern-day crisis communicator. With an iPad in one hand, a smartphone at their ear and their next tweet at the top of their mind, crisis communicators now arm themselves with the very technology, knowledge and socially savvy skills organisations are only beginning to realise *was* the future over a decade ago.

These children of the revolution are redefining the way crises are managed, wars are fought and perceptions defended. They are redefining organisational communications — one social media disaster at a time.

Communications born again, but the fundamentals still apply

Ask any bartender: a martini is still a martini whether it's shaken or stirred. It may taste just a little different, but it's still made of the same ingredients.

Communication as a profession is no different. While the digital revolution has changed the way we consume information, during a crisis a communicator's ability to *communicate* remains critical.

Whatever type of organisation they find their desk in, crisis communicators need to recognise that in the past decade the way the population has been primed to consume information has fundamentally changed. This makes *how* we communicate just as important as *what* we communicate during times of crisis.

> 🐦 **Tweet this**
> How we communicate is just as important as what we communicate during times of crisis #SMROE

Far from broadcasting into the depths of cyberspace hoping to make first contact, if you are communicating online, someone *is* listening. In fact, more people than you could ever imagine are tuning in to brand *you*.

Perhaps one of the biggest paradigm shifts arising from the digital revolution is that crisis communications is no longer just a war of words. The online and social media battlefield is now a whirlpool of text, urban slang, video imagery, animation, infographics, presentations and instant messaging.

Do you know your LOLs from your lulz? Your tweet from your post? Your Snapchat from your Viber?

Communicating with a clear purpose, in ways and places you will be heard, is the only way to connect with and influence an audience.

The art of listening and engagement has never been more important.

There is no hiding offline; with or without you, people are talking about your organisation online and on social media. From your customers, clients, shareholders, employees and the government, through to potential clients, competitors and prospective employees, the digital footprints you leave behind during a crisis write your corporate history.

> 🐦 **Tweet this**
> The digital footprints you leave behind during a crisis write your corporate history #SMROE

Your story, even during times of crisis, is now the organisation's most effective tool for achieving redemption for the digital sins committed against your audience.

Crisis communications provides an in-depth understanding of the social media landscape and how it influences your on- and offline reputation during organisational crises.

Crisis communicators are the technological storytellers of organisational nightmares.

It's all about narrative

Send your Spin Doctor into retirement.
There will be no spinning on the social media decks.
That DJ is just playing the same ol' tune … inauthenticity.

The #SocialFirefighter®

Authenticity is the holy grail of social media success. Without it, you are just another organisation peddling a product or service.

Organisations that have a clear, authentic voice and an engaging narrative build stellar brands and impassioned followings. Even in times of crisis genuine communications are valued above all else.

> ✈ **Tweet this**
> Without authenticity in social media, you are just another
> organisation peddling a product or service #SMROE

At a time when authenticity is most needed, it's often organisationally abandoned in favour of sterile rhetoric heavy with buzzwords or 'keywords' that mean little to anyone.

Traditional, old-school communicators and inexperienced corporate executives still tend to see throwing company policy down the line in 140-character bursts as the preferred response. If an organisation's legal team is let loose on communications, the messages often become even more indigestible.

And the reason organisations take this approach is simple: admitting fault, that you are wrong, that you made a mistake, is still seen as corporate weakness.

This leads crisis communicators down a path where they are instructed to construct a web of words that communicates plausible deniability. Instead of proactive media liaison, or authentic online and social engagement, fluent bureaucracy attempts to influence the perception of control and organisational solidarity.

It doesn't work. It damages your brand. And, in the long run, it's more time consuming and expensive to manage.

The worst part of this equation is the massive lost opportunity to control your narrative by engaging with your organisation's audience.

In losing your narrative to glib bureaucracy, you lose control of the way your story ends. Instead of driving your story through a logical sequence of events that follow crisis through remediation to transitioning back into business as usual, your story becomes like a choose-your-own-ending adventure book. Only you've just handed over control of selecting the way this story ends to your critics, your disgruntled social media audience and the news media.

Why would you let someone else write your organisational history?

Organisations that handle crises and social media anarchy well inspire cult-like followings and volunteer brand ambassadors. *Be one of those.* You don't need to be the next #PRFail to learn from the mistakes of others.

> 🐦 **Tweet this**
> Organisations that handle crises and social media anarchy well inspire cult-like followings and volunteer brand ambassadors #SMROE

You've just been given a free kick after the final whistle has sounded. What's your next move? Are you going to spin your social media crisis sideways? Or are you going to control the narrative and choose how this adventure will end?

The lesson here is simple: even when things are going terribly wrong, the right course of action is to keep communicating and to keep it real.

Optimus Prime: are you conditioning your audience for sales or LOLs?

Just like a Transformer, there is more to social media-based crisis communication than meets the eye. While your social stream transforms into a sea of discontent, the way you have primed your audience to engage with you *before* the crisis will play a large part in how they respond to your next move.

Are you all about the LOLs? Hard sales and bold calls-to-action? Controversy? Deviating from your authentic voice during a crisis can be tricky. Social media audiences are fickle. If they aren't learning something, laughing at something or getting a spectacular deal on whatever it is you're selling — one click and they're gone.

Transitioning them into crisis communications is just as important as transitioning them out of it.

If you can't use your usual authentic voice — humour may be inappropriate, for example, and courting controversy is an open invitation for round two in the crisis boxing ring — here are some ways you can hit that reset button.

RESET REQUIRED?

You suspect you've got a crisis brewing — some storm clouds are visible on the horizon and the forecast is for thunder, maybe a little lightning. Prepare now for what you *might* communicate in the hope you won't have to. Keep monitoring your audience sentiment and as soon as it starts to rain, issue that statement or apology.

The soft reset

If your aim is to prevent a minor crisis from escalating any further, the cap-in-hand approach may be useful. While it's more of a 'you got me there, I should have handled that differently' style communiqué, be careful not to misjudge audience sentiment and take a casual approach to genuine outrage.

The hard reset

Wish you could just start the day over? Get out of bed on the other side?

(continued)

RESET REQUIRED? *(cont'd)*

Ask your audience for forgiveness for your faux pas and let it be. Of course, you have to actually *receive* their forgiveness for this to work. Listen, engage, engage again. Gauge your audience sentiment and use poignant pauses in your regular posting cycle to demonstrate you're not ready to move on until they are.

Forget about the reset; hit the panic button instead

Trending #PRFail? Stop the merry-go-round; it's time to get off. This situation should have your *full* and undivided attention.

Forget about your online persona and just be authentic — authentically sorry. Social media outrage doesn't die down until you've demonstrated that you've heard what your audience is saying and have taken their feedback onboard organisationally. Be wary of issuing backhanded apologies or insincere statements. Mean what you say and back up your words with demonstrable action on- and offline.

MY STORY: SAILOR CREATES A TWITTER 'SHIT-STORM' IN TWEET TO THEN AUSTRALIAN PRIME MINISTER

I happened on this story as I monitored the tweet stream while working in strategic communications for the Defence Materiel Organisation. I thought at the time how well it illustrated both the impact of social media on news making and, more specifically, the role of a carefully articulated social media policy in helping organisations to defend against employee-generated social media crisis.

In days gone by, sailors had a reputation for causing chaos in port cities around the world. In their race to shake off the cabin-fever of months at sea: bars were drunk dry, brothels were bonked out and the cells of the local police stations overflowed with those who had drank the former and missed out on the latter.

In days gone by, the nightmare of 'sailors gone wild' for the ship's public affairs officer was largely confined to the local newspaper, perhaps a lucky news camera crew.

Things have changed.

Social media has made it possible for any employee, anywhere at any time, to provide the news media with both content and story.

Such was the case when a Royal Australian Navy seaman decided to tweet then Prime Minister Kevin Rudd (see figure 1.1).

Figure 1.1: a sailor's exchange with then Prime Minister Kevin Rudd

Ross Chapman @chapsax 🐦
Apologies to **@KRuddMP**. My fellow sailor has farted in that lift just before you got in. **#awkward**
7:12 PM - 24 Aug 2012

Kevin Rudd @KRuddMP 🐦
Not to worry mate. I'm in politics. Therefore by definition I did not inhale. KRudd **@chapsax**
8:56 PM - 24 Aug 2012

Ross Chapman @chapsax 🐦
@KRuddMP It appears, for want of a better word, that tweet may have created a shit storm...
9:29 PM - 24 Aug 2012

Kevin Rudd @KRuddMP 🐦
@chapsax Oh dear! KRudd

11:40 PM - 24 Aug 2012

The ever watchful media monitor the social media accounts of politicians and other notable members of the public for news, so when Kevin Rudd retweeted and then interacted with @chapsax, the resulting story was quickly published by Melbourne's *Herald Sun* newspaper, this extract of which is still online today, some three years later.

Even though the prime minister appeared to take the tweet in good humour, the media could quickly verify @chapsax's identity via his name and a correlating LinkedIn account.

Cue organisational embarrassment via vicarious liability.

Social media has given everyone a voice, and it doesn't place any caveats or disclaimers protecting organisations from becoming collateral damage to their employees' personal online antics. Being heard has never been easier, yet common sense hasn't become any more common.

We've all been slowly acclimatising to a life of consuming information in short text bursts and video snippets, but (has anyone noticed?) we're now all instinctively communicating like mimics. What we consume, we then externalise in our own interactions with the world. It's a global case study of monkey see monkey do.

So while tweeting world leaders can be considered a hobby for some, when does fun cross the line to folly? What is good humour to the mind of one person may be offensive or disrespectful to others. Where is that line between personal privacy and organisational liability on social media?

Is it invisible because a social media policy doesn't exist in your organisation?

A robust social media policy is an organisation's first line of defence against employee-generated social media crises. We'll look at some of the organisations doing this well in the chapters that follow. Your second line of defence is a well-executed training and awareness program.

How are your organisational social media defences looking?

2

Ready, aim ... misfire:
why you must be social media data savvy

What's your social media data story? Do you know?

Are your posts being read on mobile devices from the battlefields of Syria to the desktops of the urban jungle of New York? Does your audience demographic hit your target market with military precision, or are you selling surfboards to Eskimos? When is your peak posting time? When single twenty-somethings are riding the subway on their way home from work or during beer o'clock on a Friday afternoon?

If you're thinking that all has a lot more to do with social media marketing than it does crisis communications, think again.

Crisis communicators need to be able to read and drive social media data and analytics like a sales junkie on a commission high. In fact, they need to be able to read that data better than a marketer to spot discontent before it turns to outrage, and to know when to hit play, stop and pause on the crisis communications messaging jukebox.

> 🐦 **Tweet this**
> Crisis communicators need to be able to read and drive social media data and analytics like a sales junkie on a commission high #SMROE

If you're not reading social media data and looking at social media analytics as part of your overall crisis communications strategy, you are missing out on the information that will make or break your crisis remediation strategy.

You might be ready and have a good aim — but when you fire, will you hit your target audience?

The social media iceberg

Social media and icebergs are more alike than you might think: what you can see above the water — your public social media channels — is but a small portion of the iceberg entire. Underwater, where the bulk of the berg floats, is where the real social media magic takes place (see figure 2.1).

Figure 2.1: the social media iceberg

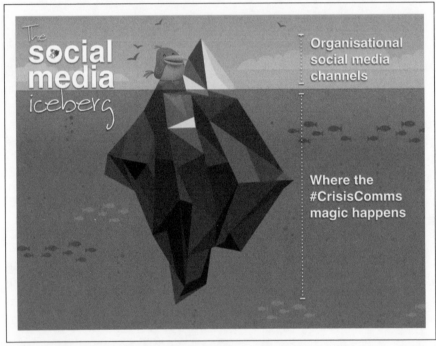

Source: Background image: © deedl/Shutterstock.com; Blue bird talking image: © Qiun/Shutterstock.com.

Much like those onboard the *Titanic* that fateful night in 1912, crisis communicators looking at the social media landscape without the information that lies beneath the surface of all social networks — their data — are steaming toward disaster.

The ability to read the social media data play is an essential tool in the crisis communicator's toolbox. This skill ensures not only that you are prepared for crisis and your strategy is correctly directed, but that when crisis occurs you aren't misfiring because of data blindness.

> 🐦 **Tweet this**
> The ability to read the social media data play is an essential tool in the crisis communicator's toolbox #SMROE

With data one of the biggest drivers of social media success, it should be of no surprise that when crisis occurs, this information becomes one of the most important resources for a crisis communicator.

By 'social media success' I'm not talking about the size of the social entourage you've amassed (or bought). I'm talking about the behind-the-scenes information that your social interactions and audience profiles generate.

For social media crisis communicators, numbers are relative. A large audience, for example, may not adequately represent your target market, and even if they do, they are useful only if they are engaging organically with your organisation.

A smaller audience may actually have a greater organic reach, because the levels of engagement can be higher with more precise targeting of your communications.

Regardless of its size, the rubbernecking and social on-boarding that occurs during a crisis can significantly change the composition of your audience. This makes knowing what your audience's data set looked like before a crisis an essential part of knowing where to focus your communications effort.

> 🐦 **Tweet this**
> Below the waterline, where your larger audience has been all along, is where you should target your messaging #SMROE

To continue the iceberg analogy, you don't want to be concentrating all your crisis remediation efforts at the top, where all the sticky-beakers have come for a gander; below the waterline, where your larger audience has been all along, is where you should target your messaging.

WHAT LIES BENEATH THE SURFACE OF THE SOCIAL MEDIA ICEBERG?

For crisis communicators who have yet to dive into the depths of social media data, let's take a brief journey into Facebook insights and Twitter analytics (as examples). Some of the most basic kinds of data gathered by being online are:

- the geographical locations of your audience
- peak post-engagement times
- age and gender aggregated data
- externally referring sites (such as your blog or website)
- how many clicks per URL in a post (further broken down into geographical regions)
- your audience's aggregated interests (both professional and personal)
- which type of post they are more likely to interact with (picture, video, text and so on).

You can see that a lot of valuable information lies under the waterline of the social media iceberg; and it's this data that will be of inordinate assistance to you while planning for, and during, a crisis.

Taking it a step further looking briefly at other social media networks, such as YouTube, LinkedIn, SlideShare, Swarm, Instagram … the list goes on, you can establish a clearly defined profile of your social media audience, and where you are being heard.

Expand the social media data equation yet again with API[1] and you have a whole new information set at your disposal, one that is driven by their

---

1. API: 'Application Programming Interface: a set of functions and procedures that allow the creation of applications which access the features or data of an operating system, application, or other service.' [Source: Google]

web browsing history and their ecommerce interactions. This information can be exceedingly useful for targeting your outbound messaging during a crisis.

And for the grand finale, on top of your social and API data, customer loyalty schemes offer another layer of personal data.

From marketeers to info ops: this will blow your pixels off

Are you ready to follow me into the data-driven future?

The data sets I've been talking about are predominately geared for marketeers. Crisis communicators and military information operations specialists can leverage the same data sets by reverse engineering them for their own purposes. Table 2.1 outlines three examples.

Table 2.1: reverse engineering data sets

Data set	Marketeers	Crisis communicators	Info ops
Geographical location	Drive sales based on location to stores.	Target audience segments for reputation remediation.	Target individuals or groups of interest to counter self-radicalisation messaging.
Peak posting times	Post strong calls to action such as sales, VIP offers and other incentives to drive and convert sales through ecommerce portals.	Using a political party as an example, if I wanted to announce a popular policy I'd post it during the peak posting times of day. Conversely, if I wanted to sneak an unpopular policy under the radar, I'd post it at the times when audience engagement is at its lowest.	As an open source intelligence tool, you can track an audience segment's online activities by watching their engagement levels at different times of the day and of the week. You can then use this to target audiences precisely for the purposes of influence or intervention.
Age and gender	Target audience sectors such as tweens, teens or young adults for specific product marketing.	Target specific audience sectors to influence positive product (or identity) trust, credibility and opinion.	Influence audience segments to build organisational trust and awareness during times of humanitarian relief.

Mind blown? It's not every day you discover that the sum of your existence can be quantified by your online engagements and transactions.

The reality is that while much was made of Edward Snowden spilling the NSA's secrets to the world, Facebook, Twitter, YouTube, Google and every other social network has been quietly harvesting, mining and storing your personal data since their launches.

It's not governments that hold the key to data mega-cities; it's social networks. And for the most part, people give away their data freely without thought to the digital footprints they leave behind — because they don't see the trail they're leaving.

Much has been written about online reputation management and the risks associated with social media profiles, particularly for military personnel, but the privacy debate that rages at the consumer level is obsolete.

People who have no end of concern about the way governments obtain, store and use data will happily sign up for a consumer loyalty card or log into apps like TripAdvisor and Expedia using their Facebook or Twitter credentials, often with only the 'promise' of reward at some time in the future.

Much like politicians' pre-election promises, loyalty schemes are built to collect data for marketing purposes, not to reward their members. You are being conditioned to develop purchasing habits through which your own data is used to market products or services directly back at you.

And I really do mean *at* you. From aggressive email marketing campaigns to social media advertisements, online behavioural advertising drives all the marketing you see online.

Start thinking about what information and social data could mean to your strategy — in the boardroom or on the battlefield.

Start thinking about having or regaining the tactical information advantage. Start thinking beyond this month, this year, this decade.

🐦 Tweet this

Start thinking about what information and social data could mean to your strategy — in the boardroom or on the battlefield #SMROE

If you are not driving your strategy toward tactical advantage now, you are allowing your competitors and adversaries to fly right past you like Marty McFly on a hoverboard.

The *Back to the Future* reference here is deliberate. Whether you are looking at corporate entities like Kodak or military actions like the war in Iraq, organisations that fail to see the value in social media data will be sending themselves 'back to the future' when the strategies and tactics of their competitors or adversaries overtake them, irrevocably redefining the boardroom or battlefield environment in the process.

So whether you are planning for organisational crisis communications or military influence, understanding the big data game plan of social media is essential.

It's no longer enough to monitor your social media networks for retweets, comments and likes. This strategy barely scratches the surface of risk mitigation or online operational acuity. At best, it will give you a skewed view of the data; at worst, it will misinform your strategy and planning cycle, leading to opportunistic misfires.

> 🐦 **Tweet this**
> Understanding the big data game plan of social media is essential #SMROE

You may have noticed that I've mentioned planning cycles a few times already in this book. You'll hear me reinforce this endlessly. Social media in the online battlespace — whether in the public or the private sector — is cyclical in nature, and your planning needs to reflect the environment in which you work.

If that is in consumer-based marketing, you need to follow and roll with your data during each campaign. If you're in personal brand management, you need to know the when, how and why of your audience engagement during events, junkets, media interactions and business as usual. If you're in the military you need to be able to assess the data for OSINT, including threats, opportunities, audience sentiment and offline influence in the physical area of operation (AO).

The narrative in your numbers: what story is your social data telling you?

I recognised the inherent story that lies within social media data early on when I was trawling through Facebook looking for criminals and their associates in the late noughties. And while my social spying days may be behind me, I still see the opportunities such broadscale data presents for a range of organisations and individuals.

For example, take your organisational Facebook page's insight tab for a spin and think about the story your data is telling you — in real, human terms like this:

> 'My name is Nicole, and I'm a 35 year old female who likes your page. I live in Melbourne, Australia. I click on your posts the most when they contain videos or when you promote posts so they come up in my timeline more regularly. Sometimes I click on calls to action that send me to your website. I don't like it when you post stupid LOLcat pictures. I'm online mostly during the morning and evening commutes. I engage most with your Facebook posts from my iPhone.'

Let's take that a step further with API:

> 'I use Expedia to research my overseas business trips and holidays. I also write reviews on TripAdvisor. After visiting these two sites, and logging in with my Facebook credentials, I tend to see A LOT more ads for travel-related products on my sidebar and in my news feed. It really annoys me and I don't click on them at all.'

I'm sure you're beginning to see not only the stories that are within your social media data but also the inherent value to you as a crisis communicator. Aggregated data tells a very distinct story about your audience segments.

Imagine how incredibly hard it would be in today's uber-connected and socially savvy world to communicate effectively, and with influence, without knowing anything about your audience. In a crisis, without knowing where to aim your social messaging, how can you be sure of hitting your target?

The key to unlocking organisational data, whether from social media, records management or the history files, is to humanise it. What's the story? Where are the personal touchpoints you and others like you can relate to?

> 🐦 **Tweet this**
> The key to unlocking org data, whether from social media, records management or the history files, is to humanise it #SMROE

Why social numbers don't always add up to Klout, influence, votes, dollars, sales and raving fans

Many people assume that those with a large social entourage (big social numbers) are at the pinnacle of social success. They command influence by simple virtue of winning the numbers game. Like a lot of things about social media, perceptions like this are often the result of a well-constructed façade: a big fancy shop window — but no customers in the store; a restaurant on one of the busiest, most fashionable strips — but no one's eating inside; a flashy car, a handbag dog, a celebrity lifestyle — all paid for on credit.

On social media, you can see accounts like this everywhere:

- plenty of fans, but no engagement
- tweeps galore, but no one is listing them
- LinkedIn connections up to the gazoo — but really, how many of them do they actually know or will they convert to business leads?

Which makes a *quality* audience far more valuable than a bought or constructed audience. Sure, famous people and notable members of the public can amass militias of raving fans, but their popularity (or infamy) is a currency that trades on their reputation. When their life is all Disney and G-rated, everything is swell. As soon as they shake that G-rated tag, the paparazzi stalks them like they're on a human safari. Today's celebrity can quite easily become tomorrow's PR disaster.

If you had sponsorship agreements with the likes of Lance Armstrong, Justin Bieber or Miley Cyrus before their respective falls from grace you were laughing all the way to the bank. But the moment their image became embroiled with drugs and scandal, by association they might as well have taken a wrecking ball to your brand at the same time their own was drained of social credibility.

Yes, they have numbers, but now people are more interested in watching the soap opera crisis than they are in them as performers or brand ambassadors.

So, whether the numbers are big or small, don't make assumptions. Until proven otherwise, assume everything is based on engagement rates. And then apply a commonsense filter.

Where are the better numbers in this equation?

Content and reputation have more value and meaning on social media than numbers ever will. This is reflected by people with impassioned followings or, as @PatFlynn likes to call them, 'Raving Fans'—people like:

- @PatFlynn
- @BrianSolis
- @QueenRania
- @MichioKaku
- @HillaryClinton
- @RichardBranson.

So if you've amassed a social entourage of raving fans, converting them to votes, likes, sales and Klout should be easy, right?

 Tweet this
Content and reputation have more value and meaning on social media than numbers ever will #SMROE

Sure. But people still stuff it up.

With one of Australia's largest followings on social media, former Prime Minister Kevin Rudd should have been a shoe-in to win the election that saw him voted out of office. But instead of priming his audience to vote, he fed them an endless stream of selfies and jibber-jabber banter.

Big numbers, huge engagement—no ability to convert them to offline results.

Conversely, big numbers and raving fans can be cultivated to action. Klout is a measure of online influence, and currently US President Barack Obama holds the world's highest Klout score: 99/100, Obama's exceptionally large and active social media streams, combined with the most popular Wikipedia page in the world has seen him win the presidential election—twice. Big numbers, huge engagement—*and* results.

The lesson here for crisis communicators? Don't believe what you see.

Social media at face value can be particularly deceptive. Only believe your own logical reading of the data play. Stack all your numbers up, from various sources, and then take a holistic look. Make your call. Do the social math.

When trying to communicate influence to remediate a crisis, you cannot depend on a social audience built on selfies to embrace your call-to-action. They simply haven't been primed to receive that kind of information. Interjecting official statements and such into the 'regular scheduling' will only confuse and bemuse them. It's a total misfire from a crisis communications point of view.

In identifying *where* your activated raving fans reside on social media—and your other online and offline channels—set your sights firmly on where you know they are. Engage them with content of substance over the long term. Condition them into responding to your calls-to-action. Give them reasons to support you. Connect with them on a human (not social media) level.

Because when crisis arises, you want activated, positively raving fans. Not people waiting for your next selfie.

MY STORY: 'BORDER SECURITY' — MANAGING AND CORRECTING PUBLIC PERCEPTION

The award-winning television series *Border Security: Australia's Frontline,* now in its 14th season, was an immediate ratings hit for the Seven Network in Australia both locally and via syndication throughout the UK, Europe and Asia.

Following the on-the-job stories of Australia's Customs and Border Protection, Immigration and Quarantine officers, *Border Security* walks the line between reality television and documentary.

The camera crew was a semi-permanent fixture on shift at Melbourne's International Airport. What went to air was edited to maintain operational security (so as not to jeopardise law enforcement methodologies and ongoing operations, or give criminals lessons in border control evasion). Each finished story, while true to the events, was compressed into about seven minutes of high-tempo screen time.

This is a formula for television and ratings success — more positive publicity than you could muster with a litter of cute sniffer-dog puppies and the creation of perceptions about 'the job' that didn't entirely match up with reality.

Yes, that's right — television and reality are *different.* Call me cynical, but how do people not know this?

What audiences saw in each high-tempo episode could take weeks of waiting around the airport to capture. Even if a story was good, there was no guarantee the passenger would agree to it being aired.

Far from finding drugs every hour of every shift, for hundreds of officers at the border, the mundane tasks of collecting revenue, charging taxes and stamping passports define their normal work-day reality. That, of course, is too boring for TV.

And then there is the small detail of being Officers of the Law, not the cast of a reality television show.

As with many of my colleagues, even when performing routine tasks like picking up a few groceries on my way home after a shift I would find that the uniform was a magnet for members of the public, who had endless questions about drugs, criminals … and the TV show. *Who did we bust that day? Will it be on TV?*

Did I resent the cameras and attention? Not at all. I'm all for using television as a medium for public education. In fact, it actually made my job easier at times, when I found people were more familiar with what you can and can't bring into Australia because of what they had seen on the television series.

What I found less gratifying were the false perceptions of the job that it created as a by-product.

One morning, while speaking to a large group of prospective recruits on the realities of working in Border Protection at an international airport, I was asked what it was like to be on reality TV – and whether the camera crew would be around during the recruitment process.

I crushed more than a few dreams of stardom that day by recounting some of the real 'highlights' of my career at the airport:

- 2 am: Together with another female officer, I'm watching a fully naked woman defecate into a controlled toilet while another member of the team is out the back ready to rummage through her faeces in search of narcotics hidden in condom pellets.

- 11 pm: I watch an aircraft approach for an emergency landing with an engine on fire. Tears of relief and the hugging of complete strangers follows when the aircraft lands safely.

- 10 am: A flight from Bali lands and the pilot requests assistance at the gate. I wait with my colleague and two Australian Federal Police officers for the aircraft door to be opened. Out comes a tall guy who kicks one of the police officers in the back and makes a run for it down the airbridge. I chase him halfway down the concourse until he runs straight into a dozen more AFP officers and ends up kissing the carpet.

- 4 am: Napping on the sofa in the staff room.

- 9 am: Find a human skull in a passenger's bag.

- 5 pm: A passenger has had a heart attack and dies at the departure gate.

- 7 am: I retrieve a partially destroyed passport from an aircraft toilet (think cistern, and many, many layers of latex gloves).

- 11 am: While searching a passenger's bags I get a whopper of an electric shock from an electrified tennis racquet cum mosquito-swatting device.

And they're just some of the stories I *can* tell you about.

As a crisis communicator, and with the benefit of hindsight, I can see the perceptions created by the TV series are simply the result of both a desire for a positively geared publicity vehicle in an area of government that by necessity has more secrets than public stories; and a commercially driven television network looking for ratings success to sell advertising space.

The lesson for crisis communicators, particularly those working with social media and online channels of organisational publicity, is that if you are using a 'behind-the-scenes' approach to content creation, be very careful about the perceptions you create. Public perceptions, whether positive or negative, will have knock-on effects in other parts of your organisation.

From recruitment to media interest to employee relations and the quality and/or quantity of social media engagement, an over-reliance on spinning a particular organisational perception can create a human resourcing overhead that may not be of commensurate value to your organisation.

Your marketing, communications and social data may be singing a happy tune, but do your engagement figures indicate a good return on investment?

3

The hurt locker:
getting inside is easy; escaping an art

hurt locker
noun. a period of immense, inescapable physical or emotional pain
(Urban Dictionary)

Unsurprisingly, social media can be both the cause of and the solution to your organisational crisis. It's an ally and an enemy at the same time.

There is no quicker, surer way to get into the media than through a #PRFail; and there is no quicker, surer way to dig yourself out of the hurt locker than by using the media to your advantage. The 'to your advantage' part is where organisations find themselves rapidly treading water in the prevailing media world of click-bait and news-for-sale.

Far from being an equal, symbiotic relationship, the traditional media's use of social media as a news-for-sale content service often ignites issues on social media in the first place, where the framing of issues lines deep pockets and a general inclination toward a click-bait mentality is geared for sales rather than truth.

> 🐦 **Tweet this**
> There is no quicker, surer way to dig yourself out of the a #PRFail hurt locker than by using the media to your advantage #SMROE

Oscar Wilde wrote in 1891:

> In the old days men had the rack. Now they have the Press. That is an improvement certainly. But still it is very bad, and wrong, and demoralising.

Somebody — was it Burke? — called journalism the fourth estate. That was true at the time no doubt. But at the present moment it is the only estate. It has eaten up the other three. The Lords Temporal say nothing, the Lords Spiritual have nothing to say, and the House of Commons has nothing to say and says it. We are dominated by Journalism.

In the intervening 124 years, ideals around the Fourth Estate have not greatly changed. There has been no evolution of the press with the rise of social and online media. This presents serious risks to organisational reputations, given the vulnerability of the 'free press' that lies in capitalist overtures with subtle (and in some parts of the world not so subtle) political and religious propaganda.

Today's journalists are in the business of producing news that is marketable. Major online news sites feed 'news' through your social streams at a rate of knots, while their website simply serves as a platform for selling advertising and associated content.

So long as advertising revenue is the first priority of a news media outlet, and news itself is of secondary relevance, organisations need to recognise that their story — in crisis or business-as-usual mode — may be framed for profit rather than truth.

Media outlets are increasingly opportunistic in sourcing much of their content from citizen journalists or armchair generals, at no cost. This is a great situation for the news media but is problematic for the rest of us. It also contributes to making crisis management a complex and drawn-out affair with numerous moving parts, not the least of which is the information you are attempting to convey.

The information vacuum: why going AWOL on social media isn't an option

2014 was the year of the information vacuum both on the battlefield and in the boardroom.

An information vacuum is created when there is an absence of credible information around a subject. It occurs when you stop communicating — or you were never present in the conversation to begin with.

An information vacuum can form because of deliberate organisational actions or positions, such as a policy of 'no comment', or simply because no new information is available to share.

From the boardroom, such was the case with the disappearance of Malaysia Airlines flight 370 in March 2014. The initial absence of any authority taking charge of the incident and providing a conduit of information created an information vacuum that was filled for a time by media speculation and conspiracy theories.

> 🐦 **Tweet this**
> An information vacuum is created when there is an absence of credible information around a subject #SMROE

On the battlefield, we saw the Islamic State of Iraq and the Levant's social media jihad succeed because the majority western military forces failed to keep their eyes on the long game. While everyone was sweating the big stuff — the Joint Strike Fighters and the Combined Arms Fighting Vehicles — they forgot about the small stuff, and social media. Such was the prevailing view of relative priorities in the military, full-spectrum dominance model that social media simply flew right under everyone's radar — with disastrous effect.

In both scenarios we, the crisis communicators in the equation, created the very information vacuums that were then used against us in the media and on the battlefield.

Which tells us one critical thing: going AWOL on social media is a *very* bad strategy.

When you are AWOL on social media, you lose the ability to tell your own story and craft your own organisational narrative. But your absence doesn't deter others from writing that narrative for you; if anything, it gives them the keys to the bus and a full tank of gas to get started with. Unsurprisingly, you are probably not going to like the stories they come up with.

> 🐦 **Tweet this**
> Going AWOL on social media is a very bad strategy #SMROE

Being AWOL on social media, which by default creates an information vacuum, gives your adversaries a distinct advantage, both in the boardroom and on the battlefield. They simply see where you are not, move in, own the narrative, and set up shop or command post.

Once your adversary is well established in the information vacuum *you* created, it's incredibly hard to regain an offensive foothold. You're constantly at a strategic disadvantage as they have built an audience, or fed a hungry news media, that has been conditioned by their actions. Until you can achieve an information equilibrium you are but a single voice singing against a chorus of their advocates.

The only way to combat information vacuums is not to let them form in the first place.

Be socially present, engage early and engage often. Identify the area of social and online media where you need to maintain a presence to mitigate the risk of creating an information void.

This means taking a very long view of your organisational planning. The move into new markets or battlespaces will require a pre-emptive entrance into the social and online domain long before the first product is sold or the first soldiers hit the ground. This requires strategy, planning and execution to ensure that you are building your village of support online long before you actually need it.

From battlefield to boardroom — the threat posed by information vacuums

In 2014, for the first time we saw the mass divergence of information in a way that created voids that were filled by fiction, conspiracy theories, citizen journalists and terrorists.

Borrowing some conceptual astrophysics from the *Star Wars* universe, think of an information vacuum like *hyperspace*. You know, that moment when Han Solo, with Chewbacca at the helm, punches his ship into lightspeed and the stars become trails of light? Social media is very much like flying through hyperspace. You've plotted your course; your destination is a long way from the Empire's armada, but nothing lies between here and there. No stars, no planets, no comets, no asteroids ... just nothing.

If you know the *Star Wars* franchise well, you'll be acutely aware that whenever Han Solo drops out of lightspeed, trouble follows shortly thereafter. Whether he flies into an ambush or discovers Jabba the Hut's bounty hunters hot on his rear thrusters, you can bet your nova crystals a firefight is about to unfold. So, knowing his adversaries' modus operandi, you'd think Han would have the strategic foresight to plan ahead for these outcomes. Of course, that hardly makes for good drama.

In a crisis communications sense, an information vacuum is no different. It's relatively easy to get yourself into a position of tactical *disadvantage*, so knowing that you're headed straight for an ambush or have bounty hunters on your tail moves you to a position of tactical *advantage*. The key to winning your next engagement, or turning the tide of a battle in your favour, whether on the battlefield or in the boardroom, is information.

Information is something you already have or will have access to as a by-product of your crisis. It's something you can plan with, and in many cases you can even pre-prepare it. So use it for strategic advantage.

Do not let an information vacuum form around your crisis.

CASE STUDIES: THREE DIVERGENT INFORMATION VACUUMS FORMED DURING 2014

The disappearance of Malaysia Airlines Flight 370 (MH370)

At the time of writing, the disappearance of flight MH370 remains one of the greatest aviation mysteries of our time. A plane full of passengers and crew inexplicably disappeared without a trace.

As the media swarmed to report any morsel of related information they could find, neither the Malaysian Government

(continued)

CASE STUDIES: THREE DIVERGENT INFORMATION VACUUMS FORMED DURING 2014 *(cont'd)*

nor Malaysia Airlines had any information to share. As time went on with no trace of the plane found, or any meaningful engagement with the ravenous press pack, an information vacuum formed and a media tipping point was reached.

Having run stories from every angle for the better part of two weeks since MH370's disappearance, and with no solid news to report, selling the story of hope became harder and the focus shifted from blame to foul play and back again.

The information vacuum created in the first days and weeks after the plane's disappearance led the media to rely on third-party content — sourced, by and large, from stories trending on social media, spun anew for headlines around the world.

With the spread of outlandish theories that had the plane located on the moon or in a top-secret United States Air Force base on an island in the middle of the Indian Ocean, the news media became a conspiracy theorist's wet dream and a publicist's nightmare.

When the focus of the search shifted to an area of ocean west of Australia, the Australian Government took a leadership role, appointing retired chief of the Australian Defence Force Angus Houston as an official spokesperson. Under his leadership the information void ended, the press pack fell into line and the news media returned to reporting developments as they happened.

The reputational damage to both to Malaysia and Malaysia Airlines had been done, though. The airline suffered not only a worst-case scenario for an airline in a crisis-management context, but also the effects of its lack of effective crisis communications flowed onto to the rest of its business.

People began to avoid flying with the airline and choosing Malaysia as a tourist destination, leading to massive financial losses across the airline business sector. Even discount flights failed to lure back enough business to save jobs.

The lesson? Take an early leadership role in your own crisis, and be heard. Even if you have nothing new to say, keeping the lines of communication open consolidates your position as a single, authoritative information source to the news media, bolstering your credibility and minimising the risk of an information vacuum. Control the press pack with regular face time and a willingness to answer questions.

The Islamic State of Iraq and the Levant's (ISIL) social media jihad

In 2014 we saw social media effectively weaponised for the first time. The terrorist group the Islamic State of Iraq and the Levant (ISIL) used social media in a tactical offensive that saw the battle lines of traditional asymmetric warfare forever changed.

With slick propaganda snuff videos in high definition and graphic photographs, ISIL have been serving up news content to the media on a silver platter.

The provision of free, high-quality news content that has shareability at its core is a masterstroke with origins in viral marketing. ISIL have exploited the news media's weakness for ready-copy-play content and have been propagating vile new content quicker than the news media and global population can consume it.

This situation led to an information vacuum forming around their use of social media. As a pre-emptive strategy, this ensured they were the only voice in the social sphere, making counter-narrative attempts, after the commencement of their social media jihad, extraordinarily difficult to accomplish.

The lesson? If you are a corporation about to enter a new sector or a hostile marketplace, or are on the cusp of reputation remediation, send in the communications team first.

(continued)

CASE STUDIES: THREE DIVERGENT INFORMATION VACUUMS FORMED DURING 2014 *(cont'd)*

If you are a war fighter, your information operations teams need to have lived and breathed your area of operation well before your boots hit the ground.

Building your authentic narrative before you arrive, cultivating a village of support and knowing the information environment you are about to enter is now more critical than ever.

Operation Sovereign Borders: The Australian Government goes into lockdown over asylum seekers

One of the current Australian Government's pre-election promises was to stop the flow of 'irregular maritime arrivals' into Australia (that is, people arriving on boats without permission to enter the country). On winning office, they proceeded to lock the media out of all information regarding their operations, the status of asylum seekers, their boats and the detention centres to which these irregular maritime arrivals were sent.

This was in stark contrast to the outgoing Australian Labor Government, who had hemorrhaged information to the media about every boat that arrived, gave the media access to detention centres and publicised the arrival of each newly discovered boat.

The Abbott Government argued that it was exactly that lax approach to the information environment that gave people-smugglers the proof of destination arrival they needed to sell seats on boats to people desperate to come to Australia. But by cutting off all information they set both the media and Australian people adrift in an information vacuum.

While the rationale behind the 'stop the boats' information campaign has its merits, shutting down *all* information around the operations does more to raise suspicions than to allay fears.

How do we know the government is telling us the truth and not delivering political spin? How do we know if the claims made by refugee and asylum seeker advocacy groups are true?

A wall of silence on the information front only makes people more inclined to distrust you, which makes it even harder for you to change their perception.

Do you see the conundrum? The government has created for itself a no-win situation inside a self-induced information vacuum. It can't release information on boat arrivals without backflipping on a contentious political agenda; and it can't change the resulting perception of distrust without appearing to backflip on its 'no information' stance.

The lesson? Don't steer yourself into a self-generated information vacuum you can't credibly manoeuvre out of. Always leave yourself a viable exit strategy.

Say something! Just not anything …

Journalists very rarely ask questions they don't already know the answers to.

When faced with an information vacuum, it's easy to retreat to life behind the corporate curtain and get lost in a sea of bureaucracy and legal advice. Ordinarily, this is time well spent. You can plan your public statements to ensure you don't compromise the organisation through any admissions of liability or by pre-empting any investigative outcomes.

Only you don't have the time, and you don't need to overthink your public statements. It's not rocket science. Your mantra should be short, sharp and concise, sounding something like this:

- Our plane is missing and we're doing everything possible to find it. We will keep you updated. The next update will be at …

- Our product is faulty and we have made the decision to recall it for public safety. If you have any questions, contact …

EIGHT MESSAGES THAT SHOULD *NEVER* FORM PART OF YOUR CRISIS COMMUNICATIONS RESPONSE

1. 'No comment.'

Like a red flag to a bull, 'no comment' is a surefire way to take you from crisis to disaster. It breeds distrust because it reeks of perceived guilt.

2. 'Our company policy...'

Forget it. No one wants to hear it. They certainly don't want to read your company policy in 140-character bursts on Twitter.

3. 'In 1979...'

This isn't the time for a walk down memory lane. Your company may have had a stellar 40-year history, but right now you're in it up to the gazoo and no one wants to hear about how fabulous your business was before the crisis.

If you still think leveraging your legacy is a good idea, I have one more word for you: Kodak.

4. 'We have no control over...'

Your lack of control is apparent. Don't remind people of this and reinforce that perception.

5. 'It's not our fault...'

It might well not be your fault, but trying to persuade people of that in the middle of the crisis is not going to work. Whether you are the lead agency or the company with the dodgy subcontractor, you are vicariously liable and the perception is you are guilty by association. Avoid using the word 'fault' at all costs.

6. 'We've had a bad week, but our performance speaks for itself...'

Redirecting focus away from your crisis and back to your legacy (see point 3) is a clear diversion. There is nothing worse than a press conference or statement that promises information on the crisis but delivers only a defensive rationalisation, diverting the messaging backward to a time before the crisis happened while asking people to look forward as if your crisis hadn't occurred.

7. 'We look forward to a renewable strategy in line with our vision that will help advance our shared interests...'

What do statements like this really mean? Now is not the time to play buzzword bingo. Hiding your message under paragraphs of self-serving platitudes won't appease an already agitated audience. Make it easy for them to hear what you're saying. Don't force them to hunt for your message. Chances are, they won't bother or it will be lost in a sea of conjecture and misinterpretation.

8. 'I'd like to take this opportunity to...'

This isn't a public relations opportunity — it's a crisis. You don't have a captive audience at your disposal for the purposes of spruiking anything. Respect the intelligence of your audience by getting to the point and then answering their questions.

Going on the defensive is a natural emotional response to handling conflict and crisis. Knowing how to communicate effectively rather than emotionally is a skill that professional crisis communicators are well versed in. Leverage that expertise early.

> 🐦 **Tweet this**
> Respect the intelligence of your audience by getting to the point and then answering their questions #SMROE

Overexposed: why trashing your brand has never been easier

You might have gathered by now that I don't subscribe to the P.T. Barnum theory that 'any publicity is good publicity'. In fact, I'm happy to dismiss that theory as a fossil that belongs to a time before radio, television, the internet and a globalised media.

You see, Google wasn't around in Barnum's days and people's living memory of a circus trickster travelling from town to town was perhaps rather sketchy. Stories didn't spread as quickly; people didn't have the freedom of movement or communication they enjoy now.

If Barnum had lived today and followed the same career trajectory, he'd be on the FBI's most wanted list. There would be photographs, YouTube footage and Wikipedia entries detailing his every con. A simple Google search would remind people of his vocation and a trail of testimonials on websites constructed in his dubious honour would recount his victims' stories. Even after he 'made good' in his later years, his Google rankings would be overshadowed by the click-bait of his scandals.

So if an information vacuum can create crisis, how does its polar opposite, overexposure, also create crisis?

Firstly, consider the information environment in which you find yourself. Brands will have a different outlook to individuals, just as corporations will have a different outlook to government.

Knowing the play in your own space — that is, what the audience will and won't tolerate — is essential. Planning for measured crisis communications is therefore critical: that is where online and social communication reigns and the digital footprints you leave behind create a (positive) generational legacy.

To understand overexposure you must also understand the human predilection for hive thinking or groupthink. This mentality, when combined with social media, can have catastrophic outcomes.

In this context groupthink is a key enabler in marketing and advertising influence to drive consumer purchasing behaviours. The danger is that a mass consumer revolt is magnified exponentially when combined with social media and can hurl you from crisis to disaster at warp speed.

So at what point do you become overexposed?

There are three strategic planning factors to consider:

1   What is the business-as-usual appetite for your product, brand or identity?

2   What product associations (brand ambassadors, celebrity endorsements and so on) do you have in place?

3   At what point in your social media cycle do you see followers, fans or likes actively disengage from your feeds?

When deciding whether to scale your communications upwards (or downwards) you must consider these three points to avoid creating an information vacuum and inadvertently cultivating overexposure.

Remember, social media is aggregative in nature. This means that if your content has a high potential for virality or a high shareability factor, it is vital that you let the content run its course before releasing new content. While this may be campaign led on a defined timeline, it may also take on a life of its own. You need to remain adaptive to the dynamic nature of social media virality to capitalise on opportunities while remaining risk averse to overexposure.

This can be particularly important if your brand ambassador or celebrity endorsement already has a high profile. You may, for example, be maxing out your consumer goodwill by using celebrities who are themselves already on the cusp of overexposure.

Crisis association is no different. If your brand ambassador is embroiled in a crisis, then consumer hive mentality will transfer that to your brand or product. People will not distinguish between the individual and the company, so you need to make early decisions around halting content or withdrawing advertising already in play as a crisis mitigation strategy.

The balance to be struck between an information vacuum and overexposure, particularly on social media, is often guided by your audience sentiment. Like a living organism, your audience sentiment should be tracked in real time across your social media channels (even those you aren't on) in conjunction with real-time media monitoring.

Your consumers are your best source of feedback. Use this to your advantage by becoming savvy with the monitoring tools available to you. While you may think these tools are expensive, so is flogging a marketing campaign to a disengaged audience or using an overexposed brand ambassador.

> 🐦 **Tweet this**
> Your consumers are your best source of feedback. Use this to your advantage by becoming savvy with the monitoring tools available #SMROE

Hashtag horror! Why things go terribly wrong

I often wonder what would have become of the hashtag had the boffins at Twitter not decided to give it a new lease on life. Using a largely defunct symbol to curate micro conversations was an exceptionally clever idea. Hashtags have become so engrained in urban culture since Twitter made them useful again that most online conversations are littered with #awesome hashtags. I have to admit I'm no exception. I've even been known to give Australia's #funniest #socialmedia #comedian and content marketing expert @JordanaOz a run for her #hashtag #LOLs.

So, unsurprisingly, hashtag marketing has become the new catch-cry of the twenty-first century. You can't launch a product without one, you can't practise social activism without one and you can't go to war without one.

Here are just a few examples of hashtags in urban culture.

Hashtag marketing horror stories:

#PRFail

#QantasLuxury

#HasJustineLandedYet

#susanalbumparty

#MyNYPD

Hashtag activism:

> #HumanRights
>
> #BringBackOurGirls
>
> #NotInMyName
>
> #Ferguson
>
> #JeSuisCharlie

Hashtag politics:

> #TeaParty
>
> #Conservatives
>
> #MakeDCListen
>
> #AusPol
>
> #UKPolitics

Take that up a level and hashtag terror is also prevalent at:

> #Terror
>
> #ApartheidIsrael
>
> #ISIL
>
> #Jihad
>
> #BokoHaram

So with #hashtag #everything on the agenda, how do brands find themselves trending as the latest #PRFail after a horror hashtag incident?

Along with the traditional ways of finding yourself in the hurt locker, pay particular attention to these potential incidents:

1 *Cumulative spelling.* UK singer Susan Boyle's album launch party is a prime example of this, with the unfortunate #susanalbumparty (or *sus-anal-bum-party*).

2 *Misjudging audience sentiment.* The social justice movement in the United States uses social media to bring attention to areas of perceived injustice. When the New York Police Department ran a campaign encouraging New Yorkers to share some warm and fuzzy pictures and stories on Twitter using the hashtag #MyNYPD, they

were quickly reminded of instances of perceived police brutality and violence.

3   *Ill-timed campaigns.* In the race back to business as usual after their CEO grounded the entire fleet, stranding tens of thousands of passengers around the world, Australia's national airline Qantas decided to run a competition called #QantasLuxury. Instead of the dream travel experience tweets they were hoping for, consumers quickly reminded Qantas that they were still in the #DogHouse.

If you're thinking, 'Well, none of that is rocket science', ask yourself why we still see examples of hashtag-led #PRFails — time and time again. The answer is pretty simple: they fail the commonsense test.

The crisis communicator's commonsense test looks at the entire landscape the hashtag campaign is going to sit in — across all channels, print and electronic, its audience segments and the brand's current consumer sentiment.

Crisis communicators are rarely embedded in marketing teams or communications departments, so it's only after the tweets hit the fan that they are called in to clean up the carnage. This makes planning for social media risk an essential element of every organisation's marketing strategy.

MY STORY: THE STORIES WE TELL: ARMCHAIR GENERALS, CITIZEN JOURNALISTS, SOCIAL ACTIVISTS AND HOW THEY SHAPE YOUR AUDIENCE'S PERCEPTIONS

One of the many memorable moments of my career working at Melbourne International Airport for Australia's Border Force (formerly called the Australian Customs and Border Protection Service) occurred late one evening when I crossed paths with a 6 foot 4 inch biker who resembled what I imagine Chris Hemsworth's Thor would look like in his mid forties (read: good!).

While bikers from motorcycle clubs strike fear into most people, I've always found them to be not only exceptionally intelligent and interesting people, but also very polite.

Biker Thor (not his real name) was no exception, only as he had unresolved child support issues he was prohibited from leaving the country, and I had the job of explaining his situation to him.

Having to break the news to a passenger that they won't be travelling because of a court order is always a delicate matter. You're never quite sure how they'll react – from shock to anger, disbelief or attempts at deception.

I thought I had this routine down pat.

I was wrong.

I wasn't prepared for what happened next. My training didn't cover this wildcard scenario.

As I began explaining to Thor about the court order I watched his demeanour change. The look of genuine surprise on his face told me all I needed to know. I'd just inadvertently informed him of a child he didn't know he had.

In a shaking but thunderous voice that reverberated around the waiting area in which we were sitting, Thor blurted out: 'A kid? Child support? What...? I've never heard about this kid before!' He stood up abruptly, paused, thought for a moment, then turned to me and said, as if to clarify his surprise, 'Do you have any idea how many women I've slept with?'

I could hear muffled giggles from some of the passengers nearby.

I smiled and said, 'I have no doubt you're a hit with the ladies and while I'd love to offer you a Scotch on the rocks and a cigar, unfortunately I'm on the job and they frown on that, so how about a chilled water in a cheap-arse government plastic cup?'

We both laughed.

Biker Thor went home with more 'baggage' than he had arrived with that evening. And I went home with a memorable true story.

Storytelling is an art that is innately human. It's how we relate to each other and forge bonds with our culture, our beliefs and our identity. Along with shared experiences, stories are one of the key elements of social engagement. Through stories we come to know more about the world around us and each other.

Social media has made it incredibly easy to tell and to circulate stories – true and false – on a global scale. Now, more than ever, we are incorporating visual elements into our storytelling – from video to pictures to infographics – and the ways in which we are telling stories are evolving in response to advances in technology.

While the way we are telling stories may have changed, the need to tell them hasn't.

What this means for social media and online crisis communications is that your story, your narrative, your authentic voice, can be both a cause of and a solution to your organisational crisis. We all have different perceptions and recollections of the same events. Each storyteller frames their stories around personal bias that may or may not be motivated by a broader agenda.

If a political or social activist were to recount my story to you at some time in the future, perhaps they would reveal a negative bias toward motorcycle clubs. If an armchair general were to tell you this story, the facts might be embellished to suit the click-bait nature of their search for that elusive four seconds of Twitter fame.

The way your story is told – both by you and by others – shapes the perceptions of audiences around the world. It can fill an information void or leave cyberspace empty.

Is your message stuck in the hurt locker? Or have you mastered the crisis communicator's escape-and-evade strategy?

4

Mission recon:
why knowing your audience is critical to success

Gone are the days when being present on social media was a choice. For many, social media is the fad that hasn't passed. It's here to stay, and if you're still debating whether or not to get onboard organisationally, the clock's ticking. Fast. Because organisations that have been trying to avoid social media have actually been avoiding the broader communications and information revolution that has occurred.

It's a revolution that your customers, stakeholders, workforce and competitors have already joined. While you've been sitting on the proverbial fence waiting for the fad to pass, they have adapted to new ways of communicating, networking and consuming information. This means your organisation is now at least a decade behind the social and information revolutions of your competitors and adversaries. And you're at risk of organisational obsolescence.

How long can you sustain a business model or military strategy that is over a decade old when your competitors have innovated to exploit the technological communications revolution? How long can you maintain a strategic advantage in your marketplace, or on the battlefield, when you are missing from online conversations?

How can you influence what remains of your traditional audience as your offline communications options disappear or are overrun by digital and social replacements? Do you even really know your audience anymore? What matters to them and what are their expectations of your organisation?

And how can you hope to be able to manage an online crisis when you aren't present to defend yourself in the court of social media public opinion?

Avoiding social media isn't a strategy toward organisational success — it's a negligent approach to the real risks and challenges facing your organisation or operation at a time when the world will simply spin on without you. As noted by General Eric Shinseki, 'If you don't like change, you're going to like irrelevance even less.'

Mission: getting to know your target audience

The saying 'If you build it, they will come' may have worked for Kevin Costner's character in the movie *Field of Dreams*, but on social media there are two problems with this mindset:

1   Simply building a social empire doesn't guarantee anyone will visit.

2   Building a social empire and attracting people to visit is effective only if they are the people you *want* to visit your empire.

If you're selling surfboards, for example, you don't want your social media community to be comprised mostly of Eskimos. However enamoured with the idea of surfing they may be, you're unlikely to sell many boards.

🐦 **Tweet this**
Building a social empire and attracting people to visit is effective only if they are the people you want to visit your empire #SMROE

For crisis communicators, knowing the composition of the audience you need to influence is critical to being able to construct appropriate messaging and content. In essence, you need to conduct some social media reconnaissance. Preferably *before* you reach a state of crisis.

Generally, I recommend building this into your social media crisis communications strategy. For some organisations, however, particularly those like the military, aid organisations and charities — which can have quite transient and geographically diverse audiences — this isn't always practical.

So, whether or not you have the luxury of getting to know your audience in the planning-for-crisis phase or during a crisis, how do you get to know the audience you've found yourself with?

The answer can be found within your organisational social media data sets.

From Facebook insights to Twitter and LinkedIn analytics, you can gather (largely for free) a great deal of information about your audience from your organisation's preferred social networks. The information you collect will give you a good indication of your audience's:

- gender balance

- age

- locations

- languages.

These resources will also reveal secondary indicators of audience information from their listing of your top external referrers (or drivers of web traffic to that social network) as well as when your audience is online (peak posting times). Knowing your peak posting times is important for two reasons:

1   You know when to post for maximum saturation and engagement.

2   Conversely, you know when to post to fly things under your audience's radar. I'm not an advocate of this strategy, but it's a tactic frequently used in politics.

Recon: pin it, IG it, tumble it ...

Don't discount the power of visually based social media networks in the crisis communications and influence equation. You should have a proficient understanding of each organisational account's social media audience with a view to tailoring communications for optimum message saturation.

It's important to note that your audiences can differ significantly between social networks. You can't compare tweeps with fans, or likes with connections, for example.

Mission: audience segmentation

If you want to exert influence, it's essential you take *knowing your audience* a step further by drilling down into the data-led details of your aggregated audience information through segmentation.

Aggregates of information group people into audience segments, for example by age group, geographical location, gender or language preference.

This shouldn't be confused with the profiling of audiences for other purposes. In a crisis-communications context, audience segmentation is simply the breaking down of an audience into the sum of its parts to ascertain the most effective ways of communicating, influencing and reaching that audience during the crisis:

* *communicating* in ways your audience will easily understand

* *influencing* by being present and engaging in social chatter

* *reaching* by ensuring your social media messaging (combined with any offline activity) saturates your audience for optimal effect.

For example, communicating with women between the ages of 25 and 34 will require a different approach from that needed for communicating with men in the 55 to 64 age bracket. Native speakers may consume information faster and more accurately in their first language rather than English (this is particularly relevant in countries where there is high migration). While some audience segments will respond best to communications via social media, others may rely on traditional offline community newspapers.

Overlooking these segments means your crisis communications will not fully saturate your audience. A lack of information saturation can have serious consequences when dealing with crises that require that immediate actions or preventive measures be initiated by members of the public. For example, communicating advice around a contagious disease outbreak, severe weather warnings or a terrorist threat requires people in specific geographical locations to take measures to protect themselves and others. Failing to saturate your audience with crisis messaging in these situations could lead to serious injury or even fatalities.

Psychosocial considerations

Using social media to provide critical information in times of war and natural disaster is becoming increasingly common. It's useful for crisis communicators to understand the relationship between the psychological aspects of trauma and the social aspects of an audience's ability to interact with their physical environment versus their social media-based environment.

It's important to note the crossover here between having an existing audience and seeking an audience.

You don't necessarily have to have a pre-existing audience to be able to create another, but you do need an in-depth understanding of audience demographics and segmentation to be able to replicate the parameters of your target audience.

By using tools such as Facebook ads and sponsored tweets, as well as the savvy insertion of your organisation into the relevant hashtag conversations, online forums and other local social resourcing infrastructure, you can build an in-situ social community.

To illustrate this, think about the idea of free speech. In some Middle Eastern and Asian countries, where civil war and government oppression have fatigued and traumatised the population, it may be a criminal offence (punishable by death in some cases) to espouse views that challenge the political regime. So if you are working for an organisation that supports a local opposition group, for example, your social media influence actions need to be carefully measured against the reality of the physical situation in which people find themselves in-country.

In the context of understanding the psychosocial factors that need to be considered during crisis communication, while free speech in person as part of a physical civil demonstration may be off the table as an option, hiding behind a nom-de-plume on Twitter may be a risk people are happy to take. So although you may not be able to create calls-to-action with offline effects, social media activism online remains a valid option.

The call-to-action so familiar on social media may not be required at all, and in fact may serve only to reinforce geographical and cultural nuances that aren't achievable. So instead, give your new social community the ability to move from activism to action in digital ways.

It could be that being a source of useful information is enough. It could be that your organisation becomes a conduit for information that is shared more broadly, perhaps in the role of global storyteller.

> 🐦 **Tweet this**
> Give your new social community the ability to move from activism to action in digital ways #SMROE

Mission: audience sentiment analysis

Much has been written about audience sentiment analysis and its uses for understanding customer behaviour, measuring social media success and social media–led prediction.

For crisis communicators, audience sentiment analysis is simply the real-time tracking of your social media audience's opinion of your organisation. It provides a statistically based overview of what the social media and online landscapes are saying about you in positive, neutral or negative terms.

Knowing the prevailing attitude toward your organisation at any given time — during business as usual, on operations or during a crisis — can be very helpful for ensuring your messaging is on target and your audience's mood is in line with your online influence actions. It can also assist in identifying early warning indicators of crisis and avert further crises from forming.

Sentiment analysis isn't a one-size-fits-all equation though.

The key to successfully leveraging the power of algorithm-led sentiment analysis is to ensure the software can and does make allowances for all the nuances pertinent to your organisation. That means sitting down with the software provider and ensuring the right kinds of sentiment toward your organisation are being measured in context.

If your organisation has an audience with particular cultural nuances around how language and tone are used, for example, these connotations could be misinterpreted by sentiment analysis software. Similarly, the nuances in how different cultures use words to express emotion can affect the accuracy of your sentiment.

Sentiment software that hasn't been appropriately calibrated to your organisation can give you skewed results. It is essential therefore that while taking sentiment analysis into consideration, crisis communications remain objective about the entire social media and online landscape before changing tactics or diverting resources.

Because sentiment analysis, like any other data set, can be manipulated.

The old 'make a lot of noise over here while we sneak one under the radar over there' tactic is easily used by motivated adversaries if you are overly reliant on the sentiment analysis available without looking deeper at the data presented.

> **Tweet this**
> Sentiment analysis, like any other data set, can be manipulated #SMROE

What you might find, for example, is that the source of agitation is just a few social media accounts tweeting prolifically. This doesn't necessarily mean they're having a meaningful impact on your target audience. Similarly, people who haven't ever bought your product or service can share opinions online, thereby influencing the general sentiment.

This means that in reality the overall audience sentiment is still positive, even when the red, angry little sentiment meter on your desktop suggests otherwise.

Crisis communicators dealing with a social media crisis must never take their own logic out of the equation when working with any sorts of data, whether generated by social media, the web or the organisation itself.

Remember, data always tells a story. So whenever you are digesting sentiment analysis, or any other form of discrete data derived from social media or online, look for the story it's telling you. What is it conveying to you behind the dashboard of your desktop? Do you have a single troll on a mission to take you down? Or is your audience really unhappy about the crisis that's unfolded and how it has been publically perceived?

What's the underlying data story telling you?

MY STORY: MULTIPLE SOCIAL MEDIA PERSONALITIES: YOU MIGHT NEED ONE

While I am the first to admit that I suffer from multiple social media personality disorder, you may be surprised to learn that it is *almost* entirely self-inflicted.

Yes, you read that right: I have multiple online personalities almost on purpose. Why? It's a strategy.

Let me start by explaining the 'almost on purpose' part.

I have a rather unusual surname. (That part I can't be held accountable for!) In fact, I've yet to come across another 'Nicole Matejic'. I may well be the only one. Which makes protecting my intellectual property essential.

Of course, running two companies necessitates that I consider their individual intellectual property protection needs as well. I also have a trademark, which again requires its own online protections.

So, in my case, having multiple social media personalities is actually a proactive strategy to protect my digital intellectual property. Because I hardly want to be known as the crisis communicator who is the subject of her own crisis because she didn't take the simple step of securing her digital intellectual property!

Think about your own circumstances, your organisation's, your client's. Should they be employing a multiple social media personality strategy? Is their online intellectual property exposed to risk?

Organisational and brand variables that should be proactively registered across social media and URLs include:

• trading name(s)

• trademarks (registered or not)

• unique product names

• new products (before launch)

• nicknames (Macca's for McDonald's)

- notable character names (Harry Potter, Colonel Sanders)
- team names (the US Air Force's Blue Angels, the Royal Air Force's Red Arrows).

Registering your digital intellectual property across multiple social media and online accounts doesn't mean you necessarily have to use each social channel; you may simply wish to park them for possible future use, or in order to prevent others from using or misusing them.

From a crisis communicator's point of view, removing the element of risk from misuse of a brand name (and any consequent guilt by association) is a no-brainer. Don't give others the opportunity to impersonate you or your brand. Prevention is so much easier than cure in this context.

If you are late to the party on this, you may find that your organisation or brand's social media handles have already been registered. This is common with popular phrases or words that aren't necessarily unique to your organisation. Or you may be unlucky and find yourself the victim of a cyber-squatter, an enterprising individual who registers social media accounts and URLs pre-emptively in order to then sell what are essentially your own digital intellectual property rights back to you at a high cost. While Instagram and Twitter state that @ handles cannot be bought, sold or traded (and other platforms have similar rules), in reality it happens frequently because without a registered trademark to fall back on or the determination, finances and resources necessary to take the matter to court, you have little right of recourse.

5

Classified:
is your enemy an adversary or an opportunity?

Even when the details of your crisis are shrouded in secrecy there is still a story to be told.

Routine government press conferences, it's fair to say, are more often than not a total bore.

While the assembled, invited media wait for answers to obvious questions, bureaucrats and political advisers busily spin buzzwords into phrases that are impossible for ministers to actually speak aloud. The obligatory history lesson and political point scoring follows while departmental staffers shift uncomfortably from one foot to the other, hoping the wall they're leaning against provides some kind of magical invisibility cloak during the impending communications debacle.

Everyone feigns interest as the speaker rambles on. When the narrative approaches its natural climax, journalists click their pens to the ready, double check their voice recorders and fire up their Twitter feeds ready for the big reveal — and instead of the answers they've waited so patiently to hear, that dirty C word is spoken:

'It's *classified*.'

The collective sigh of frustration around the room is always audible. Journalists exchange looks of pained disbelief before attempting to ask some questions. When that doesn't work, they just get up and leave.

You see, no one is questioning the security of the information. It's no secret that operational information is 'classified'. In fact, the media are not asking you for that information. What they hope for is a story that they can tell or, at the very least, an authentic explanation as to why *at this time* 'It's classified' is where the public statement ostensibly starts and ends.

Because the truth is, even when secrecy and operational security must be maintained, there is always a story to be told.

The fact that the media are assembled in a room at an organisation's request indicates that there is already some currency of information in the public domain. If it's so secret, why are you holding a press conference?!

🐦 **Tweet this**
Even when secrecy and operational security must be maintained, there is always a story to be told #SMROE

You've already lost the war of information containment, so why not start crafting your organisational narrative from the very first press conference?

Your crisis may not be a story that can be told in its entirety in the next hours, days, weeks, months or even years, but each time you invest in the information cycle with an update of value, you add a chapter to the narrative you began when the crisis began.

'While this operation remains ongoing and classified, what I am authorised to tell you is this: ...'

Social warfare: why it's not just the military's problem

Before you skim past this section thinking, 'This doesn't apply to me — I'm in the corporate sector', I want you to stop for a minute and read this:

8 January 2015
Gunmen attack French satirical magazine *Charlie Hebdo*'s Paris office leaving 12 dead, 11 injured.

If you think your organisation is immune to the social media war originating from the Middle East, the Ukraine, Russia or North Korea, think again.

While the satirical magazine *Charlie Hebdo* and its editor were known terrorist targets, the human toll of the attack was inescapable. What if it had been your organisation, your corporate office? What if they were your staff?

Regardless of their targets, the terrorist attacks we see occurring around the world in which civilians going about their daily lives are caught up have global ramifications. Every person at *Charlie Hebdo* was someone's father, mother, brother, sister, wife, husband, partner, child, uncle, aunt, cousin, lover, friend.

The social media jihad originating from Iraq and Syria by the Islamic State of Iraq and the Levant (ISIL) *is* having direct boardroom impacts around the world.

In the financial sector, legislation requires that you forensically account for transactions to detect money laundering that could be funding crime and terrorism. In the airline industry, security measures continue to be refined to ensure passenger safety.

Education providers must teach awareness of social media scams and online safety, while their students are bombarded with imagery of beheadings and massacres when hashtags are hijacked for terrorist propaganda.

> 🐦 **Tweet this**
> Social media warfare has the potential to touch every single person online. Any post. Any place #SMROE

Even those who work in the not-for-profit sector, such as religious organisations, need to remain vigilant against fundamentalist radicalisation.

Far from being the military's issue, social media warfare has the potential to touch every single person online. Any post. Any place.

Brand you: social media jihad collateral damage

It is a sad reality that in today's hyper-connected world your company, your brand, your building, your employees are all vulnerable to being used as unwilling weapons of war.

On 15 December 2014 an armed gunman seized the staff and several patrons of the Lindt café in downtown Sydney, Australia. The siege ended 16 hours later in the death of two hostages and the gunman. It would be reasonable to assume that the Lindt chocolate company was not prepared, in a crisis communications sense, for the events that transpired. And why would they be? As a food service provider, their most likely risks would be things like store fires, food-borne disease, customer dissatisfaction and corporate adversaries. In the absence of any direct threats to the organisation or location, an armed siege would have been rated as 'highly unlikely'.

In today's world, organisations in any sector could find themselves embroiled in a terrorism-related incident.

For crisis communicators this presents new challenges in an area of expertise many would be unfamiliar with. Planning for the risk of critical incidents or terrorist attack — whether targeting an organisation or its subsidiary, or using the organisation as an unwilling participant (as was the case with the Sydney siege) — will require specialist consultation.

Larger organisations, particularly those in government or the military, will have the benefit of security and intelligence departments whose job it is to manage these risks and plan for organisational response. Smaller organisations won't have the advantages of such resources.

For crisis communicators considering risk in this context, it's useful to know how to ascertain information on any such threats and how you can plan for communications in the face of such critical incidents.

Is your organisation at risk?

Establishing whether or not your organisation is at risk of a critical incident or terrorist attack is not a job crisis communicators should consider in isolation of a broader organisational view of business continuity and risk management. The best way to prepare for communications during such a crisis is by asking questions of your organisational leadership team and those in risk-management roles. Your role here is to ascertain what the likely types of threats are and to prepare for crisis communications in those contexts.

PREPARING FOR DIFFERENT TYPES OF THREATS

Known threats

If your organisation has been subject to threats of terrorism or blackmail, have some robust discussions with your executive leadership team about the circumstances and what actions (if any) were taken.

Threats by association

Brand- or product-based threats can occur when one franchisee store is targeted, for example. You need to cast a wide net when determining organisation risk. It is important to be able to separate the individual (personal) contributing factors in a particular location or store from those targeting the entire franchise, and if necessary to distinguish the organisation from the brand, to ascertain whether the threat is locally contained or more broadly applicable. This is important because communicating locally versus broadly could mean running crisis responses that involve quite different language and platforms.

(continued)

> ## PREPARING FOR DIFFERENT TYPES OF THREATS *(cont'd)*
>
> **Threats via industry/organisational business environment**
> You may be a terrorist target simply by virtue of the business your organisation is in. Journalists, military forces and defence contractors, for example, are in this category. It's worth noting that your organisation doesn't have to be physically part of the 'war' for this to occur. Simply having a contract to supply goods and services to the military, or being a journalist in the wrong place at the wrong time, may be enough to put you or your organisation on their radar.

Where to source information and support for crisis communications planning

Outside of your organisation, the most useful places to find information that will help you to plan for communications during critical incidents will be from the government departments or agencies responsible for national security and domestic incident response.

Crisis communicators need to be familiar with the jurisdictional boundaries that affect their organisation. For geographically dispersed organisations, in many countries this may involve multiple agencies and the ways in which domestic agencies work together.

Many of these agencies have community liaison officers, education and preparedness courses, seminars or other information sources that can assist you to plan for organisational threats. From this starting point crisis communicators can build their understanding of the local response landscape, and how that fits their existing organisational business continuity plans.

If the threat of terrorist attack is of particular concern to your organisation, there are government agencies that provide consultancy services, for example, to ensure organisations with responsibilities for key domestic infrastructure prepare adequately. Many private sector consultancies specialise in this area of expertise. It may be useful for you to leverage and engage these resources to identify the communications touchpoints you will need to cover in the event of an incident.

How to communicate during a critical incident or terrorist attack

I want to be very clear here that during critical incidents and terrorist attacks, *what* and *how* and *when* you communicate, particularly on social media, can help or hinder the efforts of police or military responders. Whatever your preparations organisationally, you should take the lead of the agency in command of the incident before issuing communications *of any kind via any channel.*

Ideally, your organisational crisis communicator (or another experienced person) should be embedded as a liaison in the lead responding agency's media command post. Where this is not possible, liaison and contact should be maintained throughout the incident or terrorist attack by keeping the information flow between organisation and government response agency open at all times.

The rules of engagement for organisational communicators during a critical incident or terrorist attack are as follows:

RULES OF ENGAGEMENT FOR ORGANISATIONAL COMMUNICATORS

- Your organisation is not to announce *anything* that hasn't first been publically released via the official government lead agency.

(continued)

RULES OF ENGAGEMENT FOR ORGANISATIONAL COMMUNICATORS *(cont'd)*

- It is not your organisation's place to speak with the media or make public comment about any ongoing law enforcement or military operation relating to the incident.

- Your organisational priorities should be internally focused. Families come first. Before you make any public statements, you must ensure all efforts have been made to make contact with any next of kin of employees caught up in the incident. The media may speculate, and even publish the names and pictures of employees (often lifted from social media accounts), but your communications should be focused on your people's welfare and that of their next of kin.

- The media will come calling. Give them your prepared statement and refer all operational questions to the lead government response agency's media point of contact. Now isn't a time for media or social media engagement. It's a time to focus on your people, the police and/or military officers going to their aid, and ensuring that justice can prevail.

- Trade in *facts*. Share verified, factual information from authorised sources (such as the lead government agency's social media account) to ensure your audience is kept up to date with events.

- Be human. Your social media audience will be watching your every social move, so make each one count. When sharing information, if any commentary is needed at all it should be focused on your people.

You may think, after reading this list, what do I have left to communicate if I can't control the narrative? It's a fair question, and one I'll answer from my experience in operational law enforcement.

> 🐦 **Tweet this**
> Your social media audience will be watching your every social move, so make each one count #SMROE

During critical incidents involving your organisation, you don't get to be the narrator until *after* the crisis has passed. Your priorities should be focused on — and I'm deliberately repeating this mantra to convey the importance of this messaging — *your people, the police and/or military officers going to their aid, and ensuring justice can prevail.*

While the incident or attack *involves* your organisation, it's not necessarily *about* your organisation.

Your organisation is not the newsroom for the incident or attack.

Your job is to prepare organisational crisis communications in step with the information being released by the lead government agency. Not before, not simultaneously, but shortly thereafter.

This can be challenging when you have a boardroom of agitated executives to deal with. In scenarios like this, people who are used to being in control of situations suddenly find themselves out of their depth, unsure of their purpose.

The key for crisis communicators here is to give them back a sense of leadership and purpose. Guide them toward channeling their energies inward to doing all they can to assist their employees and leading *them* through the crisis. Leaders can talk with the next of kin; they can be with and support others in the workforce. If any customers or clients have been caught up in the incident, executives should be reaching out and offering support to their next of kin too.

It is useful to pre-emptively educate your executives about the rationale for the crisis communications tactics that will be deployed during an incident.

This will ensure everyone is on the same wavelength and avoid heated confrontations when you try to rationalise a course of action to emotional people during an irrational situation.

Always keep in mind (and educate your social media managers on) what social media content is acceptable and unacceptable during a crisis. By this I don't mean your own content; I'm talking about what other people post on your Facebook page or website. Remove anything you consider unacceptable or inflammatory from your social media channels and ignore tweets and other social communications that are aimed at engaging you with user-generated content.

As part of your overall crisis communications statement, it can also be useful to warn your audience that what is posted on social media can potentially hinder those managing the response of the police's and/ or the military's ability to do their job. Encourage your audience to avoid speculation, and tell them where they can find verified, factual information.

Comments made on social media *can* affect the safety and security of those involved in, and responding to, critical incidents or terrorist attacks. The terrorists too will in all likelihood be monitoring Twitter and Facebook, and may use any information discovered to their advantage. This is particularly relevant to the posting and sharing of pictures and video of military personnel and police going about their duties.

Encouraging and educating the general public as part of your crisis communications statements is a great way to provide information of value without including commentary or speculation. Encourage people *not* to pre-empt official investigations during or in the aftermath of the incident. Such social media commentary may jeopardise legal efforts to prosecute terrorists for their actions.

In many countries, the legal system is based on the premise that a person is innocent until proven guilty. Commentary on social media can impact the prosecution of perpetrators of serious crimes by creating a judge and/ or jury bias. That is, in democratic countries the right to a fair trial often includes 'trial by a judge or jury'. Prospective judges and jurors who have been saturated with social media content and news reporting about a critical incident are unlikely to remain unaffected, making a 'fair trial' exceedingly challenging.

The key to effective crisis communications during a critical incident is to remain factual and objective. Your organisational audience will be led by your online behaviour so ensure your conduct is exemplary and that you are helping rather than hindering responding agencies.

> 🐦 **Tweet this**
> The key to effective crisis communications during a critical incident is to remain factual and objective #SMROE

Full-spectrum dominance … oh and social media

Professor Philip Taylor of the University of Leeds once noted that '…though rarely recognized in the control-freakery world of the military…full spectrum dominance is impossible in the global information environment.' It is worth making mention of the US military doctrine of 'full-spectrum superiority' more colloquially known as full-spectrum dominance, because the underlying concepts are as relevant to the boardroom as to the battlefield.

The 'control-freakery' of the military notwithstanding, Professor Taylor's point that total dominance is in fact impossible in the information environment is entirely accurate. But should total information dominance be the target, or is it better simply to pinpoint your audiences and achieve full dominance in those particular information environments?

Social-micro dominance, if you will.

The United States military defines full-spectrum superiority as:

> 'The cumulative effect of dominance in the air, land, maritime, and space domains and information environment (which includes cyberspace) that permits the conduct of joint operations without effective opposition or prohibitive interference.'

Source: JP 3-0

While it is broadly assumed that social media falls under the 'cyber' banner, the two areas have little in common in the way of behavioural context. *Cyber* relates to military-grade interactions between discrete computer-centric networks, while social media is by definition civilian and aimed clearly at social communities.

If we accept Professor Taylor's point that domination of the entire information environment is unachievable, the concept of social-micro dominance makes a lot of practical sense for both crisis communicators and military information operations specialists:

> A social media audience segment exists, by its nature, to serve a particular purpose. Social-micro dominance would therefore be achieved by achieving full dominance in a particular social conversation thread, hashtag feed, or other network curated segment.

In a military or law enforcement context, its purposes might include, for example:

- recruitment of foreign fighters
- religious radicalisation.

In a civilian context, they might involve:

- sales of a particular product
- communities that exist to educate/inform
- groups that share a common interest.

You can see a clear military-civilian crossover here. That's because social media, whether used for military or civilian purposes, is still social media, defined by the same social network structures, parameters and conversational nuances.

From a boardroom or battlefield viewpoint, social-micro dominance is quite achievable if you have the tools and resources available to target precise audience segments.

Why would you do this?

Because you want to be the dominant narrative in the information equation. Social media is now moving toward newsfeed-like purposing, and the way people consume information is once again changing to respond to how it's being served up.

Achieving full social-micro dominance in the marketplace will ensure your brand, product or service is readily seen online. On the battlefield this equates to being able to deliver information of influence precisely.

Both sectors create tangible, measurable offline impacts in their social-micro spheres. Whether buying products or seeking humanitarian aid or voting for a particular candidate, strategically moving into existing social-micro audience segments (or creating your own) is of value in both the military and civilian environments.

> 🐦 **Tweet this**
> Achieving full social-micro dominance in the marketplace will
> ensure your brand, product or service is readily seen online #SMROE

For crisis communicators in either organisational setting, it also offers a way to communicate to precisely the people you want to hear your message.

Whether you are remediating a reputation, building influence, encouraging offline transactions or providing information of value, the audiences you have at your disposal are primed, ready and willing to hear your messages.

If these social-micro audience segments feel generally positive about your organisation, you have available an influence activity catalyst: cue volunteer brand ambassadors.

So while total information dominance in the social media sphere or battlespace may not be achieveable, you don't need to aim for the world when you only need just one portion of it — where your audience is.

If you're late to the game and find yourself having to influence your way through someone else's social-micro dominance strategy, the key to achieving superiority is to employ the full range of social media tools and resources at your disposal.

Social media saturation is a game of one-upmanship. Content creation that drives information consumption is both an art (content production) and a science (data driven). Concentrate your efforts on content that is consumable with emotively driven authentic stories that influence and engage. Socially savvy audiences will very quickly decipher which accounts are providing them with the better value proposition.

> 🐦 **Tweet this**
> Concentrate your efforts on content that is consumable with
> authentic stories that influence and engage #SMROE

MY STORY: 'WE LIKE YOUR BLOG: WOULD YOU LIKE TO WORK WITH US?' — NATO

While budding singers are discovered on YouTube and models on Instagram, bloggers are being discovered for their niche content on WordPress and LinkedIn. In my case, I was 'discovered' by NATO (the North Atlantic Treaty Organization) via my blog with first contact made on LinkedIn.

I'd been blogging on social media propaganda, socialveillance and social media warfare for some time when I received a LinkedIn connection request in October 2013 with an accompanying message:

'I work with NATO's Allied Transformation Command's Innovation Hub. We're coordinating NATO's first social media massive open online course (MOOC). Would you be interested in participating?'

To be honest, at first I assumed the message was some sort of scam. It was only by chance, when I was chatting with David Bailey MBE (now my Info Ops HQ business partner), who asked 'if NATO had been in touch', that I thought otherwise.

'Oh hang on … wow!'

And of course I replied.

That single LinkedIn message has opened more doors for me in my area of niche blogging than I could ever have imagined.

From delivering lessons live to videoing myself lecturing and dropboxing the results to NATO's Innovation Hub team, I've become a familiar face on the other side of the world, among the military communities of countries I've yet to visit.

It's an incredible feeling to meet people on- and offline who have seen the NATO Innovation Hub social media training videos and who recognise me and have a keen interest in my work in this area.

As with all good social media communicators I use Skype, Messenger and email as communication conduits. Taking the online relationship offline occurred precisely a year and one week after receiving that first LinkedIn message.

The moment wasn't lost on me.

I'd been talking about social media warfare for nearly 18 months by the time I landed in the United States in October 2014. I'd written a blog in May 2013 about how cyberwarfare was in everyone sights, while social media warfare was flying under the radar.

No one took me particularly seriously, until ISIL's social media jihad started to make headline news around the world.

And that is the story of how I found myself in Norfolk, Virginia, on one of the biggest naval bases in the world, lecturing to a room full of military personnel representing the 28 nations of NATO on how social media is being weaponised by terrorist organisations.

Socially transmitted disasters (STDs): The Clap (#PRFail) is now more contagious than ever

6

Social media is a lot like sex.

It can be good, fabulous, mind-blowingly awesome: where have you been all my life? It can also be awkward, bad and embarrassing: OMG, is he still here? How do I get him to leave?

And most of all, like sex, it can leave you with unexpected surprises that aren't of the flowers, chocolates or diamonds variety.

The socially transmitted disease 'The Clap' is the applause you get from a #PRFail when your crisis goes viral on social media.

That is, people are laughing *at* you, not with you. And they're sharing the LOLs far and wide so their friends and their friends and *their* friends can LOL too. Like a chorus line of likes, tweets, pins and Instagrams, the whole sordid affair spreads across their social media accounts like a rash.

> 🐦 **Tweet this**
> 'The Clap' is the applause you get from a #PRFail when your crisis goes viral on social media #SMROE

Oh, and you're now also searchable by video, image, news topic and more on Google, Bing and Yahoo. You may feature in a blog or news channel too ... or a dozen of them.

Not the kind of organic SEO you're after?

Apart from being highly contagious, spreading from one network to another like wildfire, The Clap also bears all the hallmarks of Groundhog Day. You know, that deja-vu feeling that you've been down this yellow brick road before: the one where you thought your social media crisis had been taken care of like a wicked witch taken out by a flying house?

But no, Google gives that little groundhog's burrow a shake every now and then and awakens him from hibernation to go chasing his shadow once again. And again.

And again.

Or perhaps congratulations are in order? Perhaps you've taken a lax approach to your social media protection during your online liaisons and you are preparing for the imminent arrival of a tiny bundle of #PRFail joy?

Fear not. You can still enjoy many a social media romp without the risks.

And no, it doesn't involve joining an order of socially celibate nuns or monks. In fact, you can have as much fun as you have the organisational endurance for.

Sex Ed 101: the birds, the bees ... and Snapchat

From the stork to the cabbage patch: the question of where #PRFails come from is one that is simply answered: #PRFails inevitably come from YOU. Your organisation, and its actions or inactions.

In most cases, the largest contributing factor to becoming the latest #PRFail is a reckless organisational approach to social media risk management. Reckless in actions, in the choice of words used or in the organisational response to external factors.

But social media crisis also presents organisational opportunities: to influence change in the way people collaborate in the workplace, to demonstrate exceptional corporate citizenship and strong, altruistic leadership during adversity. You may already be using collaborative platforms such as Yammer or Trello, but regardless of the technology at your fingertips, the key driver is a pre-emptive move toward collaborative social productivity.

> 🐦 **Tweet this**
> #PRFails inevitably come from YOU. Your organisation, and its
> actions or inactions #SMROE

Pre-emptive collaborative social productivity builds a workforce of skilled advocates. By reducing reckless organisational social media behaviours through educating your entire workforce in the social media birds and bees, you turn your workplace into a socially savvy community whose skills and expertise you can leverage. Their individual, specialised business acumen will be of enormous assistance during a crisis. Add a clear understanding of the organisation's overall vision and purpose, and your crisis-ready resource team just grew exponentially.

From the CEO to the mailroom clerk, assume there is a quantum knowledge deficit with regard to social media in your organisation and build your educational awareness program upward. Keep the social media birds and bees narrative simple and informative.

SOCIAL MEDIA 101

- What is social media? How and why do people use it?

- Which social media networks are most used within the organisation? How do they work? What is their purpose?

- What are the dangers of social media—from an individual perspective through to organisational impacts.

- How does your organisational social media policy fit into your employees' everyday working life. Case studies and examples are essential to contextualise issues and consolidate conceptual understanding.

You must also take into consideration cultural, geographical, literacy and accessibility issues.

SOCIAL MEDIA 102

- Are there cultural nuances in your organisation or workforce that you need to accommodate or provide clear guidance around? From having your awareness program available in multiple languages to offering face-to-face sessions, what is the best way to communicate this information to your stakeholders?

- Do you face any geographical issues in delivering social media awareness training? Is your workforce geographically remote, or perhaps literally at sea with limited internet connectivity? How will everyone receive the same training in a timely manner?

- Accessibility for the visually and hearing impaired is essential. Think about audiobook-style versions of any print or online content. Ensure that any videos produced have subtitles in the languages your workforce is fluent in.

When considering how best to deliver large organisational awareness and training packages, tapping into what you *already know* and what you're good at is a no-brainer. Employ internal tools that are already in use, such as Yammer or Trello. Run your awareness program as if it's an internal marketing campaign suited to the audience segments of your internal workforce:

- Mix up your content: think about infographics, video and animations.

- Mix up the conduits of information delivery: consider social, online (intranet) and offline (print).

- Use newsletters and other publications to reinforce your messaging.

- Use email marketing tactics to educate incrementally.

- Hold an online Q&A forum to encourage members of the workforce to discuss areas of social media policy or guidance ambiguity.

The more time and effort you invest in educating your workforce about how social media crisis occurs and how it can be prevented, the less likely you are to have a spontaneous, internally ignited #PRFail occur.

Investing in your people before a crisis develops gives them the opportunity to invest in you and the organisation. It's not hard to imagine the amount of power and goodwill a thoroughly engaged, happy workforce brings to the crisis communications table when the only thing you're hearing is 'The Clap'. Make sure your workforce is working *for* you, not against you, during times of social media crisis.

> 🐦 **Tweet this**
> Investing in your people before a crisis develops gives them the opportunity to invest in you and the organisation #SMROE

The Clap: are you at risk?

If you're on social media, or even if you're not, you are at risk of catching The #PRFail Clap.

I've outlined an approach to reducing the risk of catching it, but it is also important to identify organisational and individual behaviours that are early warning indicators of an outbreak of The Clap.

Organisational and individual apathy

Whether this apathy is toward the process of planning and practising crisis management, communications activities in general or a broader hostility toward social media, such negativity will only exacerbate internal organisational perceptions when a crisis does occur.

Social media crisis communicators must advocate being actively engaged in building a positive perception of the capabilities of social media within their organisation, while also recognising the blockages particular individuals will cause during a crisis. Don't plan to bypass these roadblocks. Organisational hierarchical structures will often work against you in such circumstances, particularly at a time of heightened tensions.

Confront these roadblocks to success *before* a crisis occurs and influence decision makers toward a more amenable position. Crisis will serve only to reinforce fear among social media non-believers, so take a positive approach early and repeat your advocacy mantra often.

Make social media matter to the non-believers by selling the virtues of engagement, risk mitigation and narrative control. Talk with them in a communications currency they understand.

Data blindness

If your social media data is telling you that people are unliking and leaving your social feeds, or your social traffic has dropped off significantly, it's time to look at:

- the possibility that someone has created an alike social media brand presence and is stealing your social media traffic via click-jacking or like-farming. Keep an eye on your 'own social patch'. This is a critical risk mitigation activity in protecting your intellectual property and ensuring your audience isn't lured elsewhere. Don't become an easy target by failing to secure your digital intellectual property.

- your content. Are you driving people away with controversy? Poorly delivered humour? Inappropriate newsjacking?

Take a critical look at what you might be contributing to the social media crisis equation. A change in tactics and communications might be due.

> 🐦 **Tweet this**
> Don't become an easy target by failing to secure your digital intellectual property #SMROE

Risk-taking behaviour

Risk-taking behaviour on social media may be explained by a lack of executive buy-in or oversight, a poorly trained or under-resourced social media manager, or a combination of the two.

Organisational under-resourcing

If maintaining your organisational social media presence is an adjunct of someone's job — if, that is, it's not their first or only priority — you are increasing the risk of social media failure.

Not only will employees feel conflicted (or even guilty) about the way they approach and dedicate time to organisational social media, but not having the necessary resourcing or time to moderate and measure your social media presence is akin to flying blind.

You're missing out on the opportunities and information your social media audience offers your organisation. At the same time, you're sending a clear message to your workforce (and audience) that social media isn't important to the organisation, ergo neither are their contributions toward or interactions with it.

Failing to moderate audience commentary

If you let threads of commentary get out of control you risk losing control of your own social narrative, which means you'll be automatically playing defence when a crisis occurs.

A lax approach to community moderation can lead to conflicts with the law, industry codes of conduct and governing standards. The expectation of social-media moderation has become clear over the past few years. In many cases, social media communities fall under the same guidelines, censorship and industry codes of practice that apply to advertisers. In addition, you are required to adhere to the governing laws of the country in which you operate.

Failing to adequately respond to social media comments, questions and remarks

Nothing annoys people more than being ignored. Don't provoke them with slow (or no) response or poor customer service.

Are your social media streams crossing over into the realm of customer service? If so, how are you managing multiple organisational interactions with individual complainants? Are your social media staff trained in customer service, and are your customer service team socially savvy?

Is your social media customer service aligned with the type of organisational customer experience you are known for?

Deliberately being provocative with your content

The old 'shock and awe' social tactic polarises audiences and generates wild swings in audience sentiment toward your organisation.

It's incredibly hard to keep up with a love–hate mentality toward a brand. It's exhausting from a communications perspective and will fatigue your communications team before the crisis has even truly begun.

Worse still, your audience is constantly receiving mixed messages, creating the perception that your organisation is incompetent.

No organisation has ever been able to adequately explain to me how deliberately cultivating controversy presents their brand in a way that is authentically and positively engaging.

This includes faking controversy for publicity. Not only are social media audiences fatigued by the rate of #PRFails but they can also smell a PR newsjacking rat at three tweets. Do you want to be known as the organisation that deliberately orchestrated their own #PRFail?

Failing to deploy social media protection measures

Or deploying them and then ignoring them anyway. If you don't have the tools to monitor your social media accounts in real time, away from the office, in a 24/7 environment, you are creating an environment in which failure is an imminent risk.

Social media is not a 9 to 5 proposition and your attention to it shouldn't be either. Trying to play the 9 to 5 when your audience plays 24/7 means missing early warning indicators and waking up to a full-blown crisis that could have been averted if you were timely in your response.

If you can't give the proper attention to your social media channels from within your organisational workforce, hire a contractor or social media agency to take care of this element of your business properly.

Coitus interruptus: not an effective method of Clap control

If you (or your client or employer) think that pulling the plug on all your organisational social media networks right before the big #PRFail climax is a good Clap avoidance strategy, think again.

Social media withdrawal simply isn't an effective measure of Clap control. By the time your crisis is billowing smoke, it's too late. People have taken screenshots of your #PRFail and are posting, tweeting and pinning them all over the internet.

> 🐦 **Tweet this**
> Social media is not a 9 to 5 proposition and your attention to it shouldn't be either #SMROE

Hitting delete simply isn't an option. Even if you did erase your corporate digital footprint, the evidence remains for all to find on Google in perpetuity.

In fact, like brand bashing, attempting to wipe your digital footprints off the carnage left in your corporate wake smacks of a cover-up. In times of crisis, giving people reasons to distrust you simply invites further suspicion, which will only add to the perception of organisational incompetence and untrustworthiness.

Approach the decision to delete particular posts with great caution. Rather than trying to hide poor audience feedback or organisational mistakes, take these instances as opportunities to demonstrate exceptional customer service and provide outstanding customer social engagement.

The only scenarios in which posts or comments should be deleted (after taking screenshots as evidence) are:

- *if a breach of OPSEC or operational security has inadvertently occurred.* This might involve the posting of pictures that weren't cleared for release and pose a direct threat to the safety and security of your workforce.

- *if commentary is running into unlawful territory (as governed by local, state, federal or in some cases international authorities).* This might involve hate speech, incitement to violence, discrimination, vilification or depictions of abuse. This list is not exhaustive.

- *if commentary is bullying or harassing in nature.* The last thing you want is for a verbal altercation to take place against your organisational backdrop.

Crises that are handled professionally and quickly are more likely to remediate reputations positively than crises that are handled with communications disdain.

Practise safe social media — it's all about using protection

Just as with sex, practising safe social media is a 99 per cent effective method of Clap control. And the good news is that social media protection is easily deployed regardless of your organisation's size or management structure, or the industry in which you conduct business.

The three pillars of social media crisis prevention are:

1   people

2   technology

3   corporate governance.

> 🐦 **Tweet this**
>
> Just as with sex, practising safe social media is a 99 per cent effective method of #PRFail control #SMROE

People

In social media crises, your people are both your biggest asset and your riskiest point of failure.

Social media crises are not just issues for the communications, marketing, PR or military STRATCOM team to fix.

With the most likely event being a crisis of your own making, taking a whole-of-organisation view toward mitigating risk means educating all staff, from the CEO to the mailroom clerk, on what your organisation considers appropriate and inappropriate use of social media.

Your social media policy needs to clearly articulate the boundaries of social media use, both in the workplace and privately, and the likely consequences for employees of engaging in social media misconduct.

This approach to social media policy awareness should be consolidated at all touchpoints of workplace induction and ongoing training and development. Aligned internal communication activities should periodically remind employees of their obligations when using social media.

If you don't have the organisational resources to manage your social media channels effectively, contract them in. Don't let resourcing become the reason your people fail, because the reality of that situation is that *you* as an organisation will have failed them by not giving them a fighting chance.

Technology

There is an incredibly diverse array of tools available online to assist organisations not only in managing their social media in a business-as-usual capacity, but also in being proactive in identifying and managing social media crises.

Far from being just platforms to post, tweet and share with, solutions such as Hootsuite (and their uberVU platform) give you the ability to track consumer social media sentiment in real time, see when your audience interacts with your social media content in the context of comparison with other marketing initiatives (such as television advertisements), and even drive app- and web-based engagement.

I personally use Hootsuite for corporate clients. Military organisations should explore the benefits of the RepKnight platform. Each has been specifically designed to capture social chatter in a way that can be analysed in real time and in relevant contexts.

Corporate governance

One of the most common examples of organisational incongruence I see as a crisis communicator is the setting of rules that are never enforced. There is no point in putting in place systems to ensure your people are trained, educated and equipped with the technology that will assist your organisation to avoid and respond to a crisis, if you don't enforce those policies when misconduct occurs.

It's like the corporate version of a child throwing a tantrum and the parents simply giving in instead of disciplining them. It sends the wrong message to the rest of your workforce: it says you are not consistent in following your own rules, so why should they be?

Only in the corporate world the stakes of failing to follow through on governance are significantly higher. Failing to take action on social media misconduct, for example, can lead to workplace bullying, harassment and other behaviours that are not aligned with your vision or code of conduct and may in fact be illegal in your country.

Behaviours that are a source of internal crisis often lead to external crisis. They also take more time and effort (and expense) to remediate than managing the issue correctly and inline with your policies in the first place.

Click-jacking — not as pleasurable as it sounds

Click-jacking or *like-farming* refer to the activities of entities that devise ways to steal or profit from your legitimate social media traffic.

Click-jackers and like-farmers may, for example, run a series of ads on social media promoting a competition giving away your goods and services, then direct the links to a third-party website instead of your website. In essence they are duping your customers into believing they are you.

For example, a click-jacker might set up a fake social media account to impersonate you. Your customers mistakenly believe the fake is your authentic account and start transacting with the impostor.

Facebook like-farmers in particular profit from their deception by creating fake communities that are then on-sold to unscrupulous marketeers as ready-made Facebook pages.

Click-jackers and like-farmers have a range of motivations, apart from simply causing organisational crisis and duping consumers.

BY WAY OF SOCIAL DECEPTION ...

Data harvesting

Personal data is exceedingly valuable to scammers. In diverting legitimate traffic they can amass large amounts of personal data for particular sectors. This is especially pertinent, for example, when a social media call-to-action requires you to 'Like' a post, share it and then visit a website and enter your name, address, phone number, email and other personal information.

Redirection to nefarious payment gateways

If your brand is in the business of selling products or services direct online, being click-jacked could mean your customers are handing over their money to someone else. The social media or online advertisement sends them to a payment gateway that looks exactly like yours (or close enough to fool most people). Customers will then hold you accountable when they don't receive what they paid for.

Espionage

Cyberwarfare, or targeted espionage (from within your organisation or externally), may also employ click-jacking methods that will steal/redirect/siphon your social media and online traffic. The aim of espionage is to cripple your online and social media capabilities: this can result in share market price drops, for example, and more broadly cause a loss of consumer confidence.

The only way to stay one step ahead of click-jackers and like-farmers is to actively monitor your social media traffic and be situationally aware of any new accounts opened in your name.

Platforms such as Twitter and Instagram allow only a single shot at each' username. However, it is possible on Facebook, for example, to create a Page that is identical to that of a major brand.

Using apps such as Mention to alert you to terms, keywords and trademark violations in real time is a savvy way for organisations and crisis communicators to manage the ever-evolving social media stratosphere.

MY STORY: MY GOVERNMENT-SPONSORED XXX-RATED EDUCATION

I'm one of the small number of Australians who can claim they really did receive a 'free' government education – at least in the XXX-rated sense. Yep, I've seen more porn than I care to recall and know a thing or two about kink, fetish and all manner of strange perversions.

Really, it's not half as exciting as it sounds. In fact, some of it was simply abhorrent and sleazy. Illegal and objectionable are other words that come to mind.

Airports are curious places to work. You do see some seriously out-there stuff. And during my time as a Customs and Border Protection Officer working at Melbourne International Airport, I thought I'd already seen it all.

Turns out, my first desk jockey job would prove my 'just-try-and-surprise-me' theory very, very wrong.

In 2010 the addition of a single word, 'pornography' ('illegal' was added later after all the commotion), to the Australian Immigration Incoming Passenger Card (see figure 6.1) resulted in a deluge of letters of outrage to the Minister for Home Affairs.

Figure 6.1: the Australian Immigration Incoming Passenger Card, now amended.

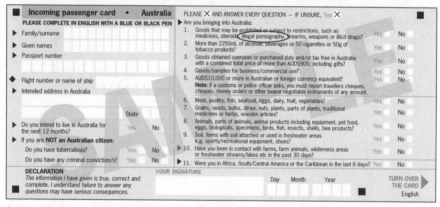

Source: © Commonwealth of Australia 2014; 15 (Design date 11/14).

Public outrage directed at a minister is in itself nothing new, but generally constituents' communications tended to be of the G-rated variety. Not this time. Some messages were barely R-rated; most were explicitly X-rated.

 <<-- that was me.

Cue my shock/horror/surprise. OMG...that is *so* not what I expected.

As I sat in my Canberra office wondering how I'd ever manage to construct talking points for the Minister that wouldn't require him to say *sex, porn, kink* or *fetish*, I had a very distinct 'Toto, I've a feeling we're not in Kansas anymore' moment.

Peculiar circumstances require a change in tactics and outlook on issues. Form letters weren't going to do the trick. There was no one-size-fits-all solution. It was a crisis of epic proportions. And the worst part was I wasn't even allowed to use any humorous puns in the departmental responses. Talk about a missed opportunity!

In all seriousness, some letters were so abhorrent that in drafting ministerial responses I felt compelled to place cover sheets on each file to warn the clearing officer about the content contained within. Those were the days of discussions about sex and porn that I never thought I'd be having with ministerial advisers and deputy CEOs.

So how do you remediate an X-rated or controversial crisis? There are a few differentiating factors that are useful to know when formulating responses to constituents or customers whose communications are not of the G-rated variety:

- *Sort correspondence into two streams — one that requires a response, the other that doesn't.*

  There's no rule that requires you to respond to any correspondence you receive; if it doesn't fit within the remit of your organisation, file it in an appropriate place — and by that I don't mean the bin — I mean in its own special place where it will never see the light of day again!

Be guided by your organisational policy on this.

If you do choose to respond, make sure there are valid return contact details to send your response to: no point wasting your resources on writing a response when you've no way of delivering it.

- *Understand from the outset that there is a level of provocation occurring.*

People write emails, letters, tweets and posts for all kinds of reasons. Some are bored, some are angry, some just like writing letters. Some are angry at something else and you just happen to be in the frame at the wrong moment. Some people are vexatious: they like the drama and they'll do almost anything to feed the troll within. Leave those people who are just looking for a fight to find it somewhere else.

- *Understand that it may not matter what you say (or don't say); some people will never be satisfied with your response.*

You can't rationalise with irrational people. No matter how 'right' you may be, or how logical your response, they will never see things your way, just as you won't ever see things through their world view.

Don't waste your time. Pick your battles. This isn't one of them.

- *Throw any ideas of form letter responses out the window.*

Emotionally charged, dynamic situations require a sincere but brief response. You might start and finish your letter with standard paragraphs, but you need to respond to the questions put to the addressee directly to avoid fanning the flames of discontent further.

Don't give people an excuse to reply to your correspondence. Your aim is to shut it down, not create a new office pen pal.

- *Read the correspondence with a highlighter in hand.*

Skim past the x-rated rhetoric and highlight the actual questions you can answer.

Don't buy into someone else's emotional world view. Simply respond to the questions that are within your remit to answer. Don't make your response personal.

Be helpful. Be honest. Be concise. If a question cannot be answered, say so. Don't leave unanswered questions hanging about like the elephant in the room. It only gives them a grievance about which they can write to you again. (Refer to point 4 about office pen pals.)

- *Got a recidivist on your hands? Call it. You're done.*

Some people love getting mail or email. Some people have a lot of time on their hands. So unless you plan on hiring in extra resources to give them a full-time pen pal, say your piece and then inform them you won't be corresponding with them any further. If they keep writing, ignore them. They will find a new pen pal soon enough; if not, buying a filing cabinet just for their mail will be a lot cheaper than hiring a pen pal just to deal with them.

The most important thing to remember during times of letter and email writing crusades, is that if you fail to respond appropriately you will only infuriate a complainant further. This carries the risk that they will move their correspondence from offline to online, and publish your response along with it.

Whatever your response, make sure you're happy for those words to be front-page news or blog fodder.

Target acquired:
social engineering and what it means for you and your organisation

7

Let me preface this chapter by saying that neither the CIA nor the FBI, NSA, ASIO, ASIS, KGB, Mossad or DoD have tracked your purchase of this book.

Well, that's to the best of my knowledge … I mean, how would I really know? Heck, they could be watching ME!

Feeling a little paranoid? Sorry about that. Well, actually I'm not.

Because you *are* being watched.

Just not by any of the aforementioned agencies — unless you're a person of interest, a criminal or a terrorist, in which case, best put your tinfoil hat back on.

You *are* being watched. By your supermarket. Your airline. Your pharmacy. Your bank. Your insurer. Your telco, eBay, Amazon, Facebook, TripAdvisor, LinkedIn …

For reasons of space, my editor suggests I don't give you the full list of apps, social networks and loyalty schemes you are being monitored by. Suffice to say, almost every digital interaction you have online (and some offline) results in your actions and decisions being stored and, in many cases, data mined to create a profile of your spending, banking, holidaying and recreational habits.

> ✈ **Tweet this**
> You are being watched. By your supermarket. Your airline. Your pharmacy. Your bank. Your insurer. Your telco … #SMROE

In my line of work, this kind of data grab is known as *social engineering*, and for crisis communicators and military information operations planners it has as many uses as it does risks.

Stalkerbook ... I mean Facebook

Perhaps the most insidious social media network for social engineering is Facebook, which also happens to be the most utilised social network on the planet.

Without wanting to sound like a conspiracy theorist, the fact that the largest social networking platform in the world also happens to house the most personal data on citizens around the world makes it a goldmine for everyone from marketeers to spies.

Have you noticed, for example, what happens when you add a 'Life Event' to your Facebook timeline? Perhaps your partner has just popped the question and you've updated your status to 'Engaged', or you've just welcomed a baby into the world. It's no coincidence that the ads now showing in your Facebook feed are centred on wedding planning, bridal gowns and honeymoon destinations; or on new baby products, retailers' baby loyalty program invitations or nappy discount offers.

For crisis communicators, remediating a reputation has never been easier. You have the ability to target your communications to your audience segment and to start rebuilding consumer trust with carefully crafted messaging and calls-to-action.

Facebook, if that's where your audience reside, is an easy mark for crisis communicators with dollars to throw at promoted posts and advertisements.

> 🐦 **Tweet this**
> For crisis communicators, remediating a reputation has never been easier #SMROE

In another stroke of social luck, you also have the ability to outspend your competitors and dominate the social media airwaves at a time when they will be trying to carve out a large chunk of your market share for themselves.

Did you know Facebook gives you the ability to spy on your five biggest competitors' pages to track their posts, engagement levels and audience size? True.

Conversely, if you are a crisis communicator and your client's competitor is riding the #PRFail wave, opportunistic messaging can capture market share and build brand loyalty for *your* brand.

You also have the ability to force your competitors to spend to keep up with your social media activity.

For military information operations planners, influencing the hearts and minds of your target audience has never been easier. You can now reverse engineer what was built predominately for marketing purposes to build influence, hit precise target groups and conduct MILDEC (military deception) operations to steal your adversaries' social traffic.

Whether you are in the military or corporate world, the big data play behind your Facebook page and the tools available to you to target your audiences are so sophisticated and so effective that *not* using these tools as part of your crisis communications strategy would be folly.

This degree of social engineering isn't confined to Facebook. You can track hashtags on Twitter just as effectively using tools such as TweetReach.

Even if your organisation isn't on Facebook, it remains a useful tool. If you can define your audience into clear segments (and you have a reasonable belief that the people you want to reach are on Facebook), you can still run ads that send clicks off-site to wherever you wish.

Socialveillance: who *is* watching you online and why you should care

Who is watching you online? Well … pretty much everyone.

I'm serious.

From the boffins behind the social media network you're using to your government to foreign governments to the pages and apps you interact with — every single touchpoint of your online existence leaves behind a trail of digital breadcrumbs that paint a data picture of you, your brand or your organisation.

Civil libertarians around the world feign outrage about online privacy, while espousing their views on the very social media networks they attack. The reality is, even if your social network of choice is locked down like Fort Knox, you are still giving away key elements of your privacy by simply being socially present and engaging in the online conversation.

It's a trade-off most people accept.

So why should you care? Perhaps you shouldn't. If you're not fazed by the covert intrusion on your privacy, individual or organisational, then tweet and post on. But if you do care, or you're in the crisis communications game, what do you need to know about socialveillance?

Socialveillance is like a Trojan Horse you invite inside: when you connect your apps to your Facebook or Twitter account (such as via one-step login). It seems harmless enough, and it can make digital life a little easier.

But, as the people of ancient Troy discovered, letting a gift horse through your front door without reading the fine print on the delivery docket can lead to disaster. Connecting your social accounts to third-party apps can leave you unwittingly exposed to cyber infiltration and ongoing socialveillance.

This is great news for corporations on the hunt for big data and savvy ways to market to customers via API. For individuals it means you're constantly bombarded with third-party marketing of products you've recently researched or bought online.

For crisis communicators, socialveillance, like the original Trojan horse, can give you a critical strategic advantage — or a disadvantage, depending on how well you've planned your invasion.

Sneaking in that Trojan Horse

If you are a crisis communicator with a range of social media data-mining and analysis tools at your disposal, you can create crisis-mitigating strategies based on real data and audience segments. This means you can communicate with influence and hit your target audience precisely.

The Trojan Horse: epic fail

Guesswork marketing is headed for extinction. Marketing science is maturing to a point where social data will form precise profiles of consumers, voters and even social influencers.

Companies will be able to gauge with statistical precision the likelihood of your purchasing their product or service, or of your voting for their party at the next election, based on your social data set.

How you use, protect and, dare I suggest, *share* this data can produce social media success or crisis. Customer outrage is seldom an isolated affair; the cost to an organisation caught misusing, selling or inappropriately profiling social data will be *epic*.

With social commerce now a part of everyday product and services purchases, the generation of social data may become more valuable than the transaction itself.

This may lead to all manner of marketing tactics where a product is heavily discounted because it's not your cash they're after: it's your data.

White collar blue: espionage and hacking is a corporate problem too

Far from being a discipline confined to the spooks of the CIA, MI6 or the Mossad, espionage and hacking in the era of social media now involve targets firmly painted on the backs of private individuals and organisations around the world.

From a crisis communications perspective, what used to be called a hostile corporate takeover can now have offline market preludes such as data hacking, resulting in adverse media and share market ripples. Hacking and the publishing of hitherto confidential or secret information manipulates the news media cycle, while public perceptions play out on social media and *then* in boardrooms.

Sony Entertainment found this out the hard way when their cybersecurity was breached by hackers in 2014. Having stolen an estimated 100 terabytes of data and leaked communications, emails and other sensitive information to the press, the hackers then demanded the cancellation of the comedy movie *The Interview*, which depicts the assassination of North Korean dictator Kim Jong-un.

The hackers then threatened a terror attack on the movie's scheduled premiere in New York City. Sony met the hackers' demands, but later released the movie straight to web.

Crisis communicators should take a leaf out of the crisis mindset of US President Barack Obama in managing crises that arise as a result of hacking or cyber espionage. Being organisationally embarrassed is one thing, but having demands made and then threats levelled is an entirely different form of crisis communications. It clearly shifts the narrative from the domain of crisis communicators to law enforcement negotiators.

> 'We will respond proportionally and we will respond in a place and time and manner that we choose.'
>
> *Barack Obama*

Crisis communicators, and the organisations they work for, should step back when an attempt at extortion or threat of terrorism arises. Negotiating in such a case isn't a crisis communicator's role — it's what law enforcement agents are trained for, and for this reason they should be alerted early and their advice in managing the crisis followed.

In 2014 we saw other ill-timed leaks of information that caused organisational grief.

When Apple's iCloud was hacked and the personal and very private information of some of its celebrity users leaked, the timing was precise. A week before the company's launch of the iPhone 6, and the same day as its rival Samsung launched its new smartphone, the internet was flooded with leaked information, resulting in a share price plunge.

Apple crisis communicators experienced a quadruple whammy that day:

- a major security breach
- leading to a serious breach of customers' privacy
- a week before a major product launch
- with serious stock market implications.

Which crisis to tackle first?

Undoubtedly (as with any crisis) the place to start is dealing with matters pertaining to people — in this case, the serious breach of customer privacy.

Finally, in a case of government espionage, Iranian hackers used fake social media profiles to get close to US military and government officials, in an operation that apparently ran for several years.

The social 'trusted insider' is an easy game to play, and the only clear line of defence for organisations is to rely on their employees to vet potential new friends, tweeps and contact requests carefully. But we all know that, in reality, it takes little (if anything) to convince someone to become your new connection on LinkedIn or your latest Facebook friend.

Organisational education and awareness campaigns are a crisis communicator's biggest asset in seeking to prevent such incidents from arising. However, in the event of a crisis, the organisation may not be able to provide much information publically because of legislation surrounding employees' rights to privacy.

In crises like this, your story is in the event, not the person — so reframe your organisational response to provide information on what you *can* talk about, not what you can't.

MY STORY: 'I KNOW THE CIA IS WATCHING ME.'

During my Customs and Border Protection days I met a passenger who had convinced himself that the CIA was watching him. I have no idea if he was on the money or not. He was absolutely certain he was under surveillance though, having arrived at this conclusion after flying back into Australia following his first trip overseas to be met by a Customs and Border Protection officer who enquired politely if he had enjoyed his holiday.

Apparently that was one question too many and he started a letter-writing campaign to everyone from the Prime Minister down. Not satisfied with the responses provided by every layer of government, he then wrote to request a copy of his 'intelligence file'. Of course, no such file existed, which only fuelled his suspicions.

I'm not sure if he gave up or decided we were all part of a larger conspiracy but, as in crisis communications, sometimes there comes a point when nothing you can say or do is going to allay someone's suspicions or change their mind.

And therein lies the lesson: changing the opinion of one person, on- or offline, may be irrelevant to the broader crisis at hand. Where individuals create their own crisis, one that isn't impacting on anyone but them — and your staff, who are fast becoming their new pen pals — call it quits and disengage.

If this army of one is having an effect on others, is it of any relevance? If they are having a quantifiable impact on your audience, then you are going to have to explore other means of communicating with them. Lawyers, the police or perhaps even mental health professionals may be needed to ensure they receive your message along with the care they may need.

Don't underestimate the army of one, but don't fall victim to their antics when their only captive audience is you.

Social media information operations:
much more than military propaganda

8

Information operations and warfare, also known as influence operations, include the collection of tactical information about an adversary as well as the dissemination of propaganda in pursuit of a competitive advantage over an opponent.

RAND Corporation

From the battlefield to the boardroom, in online and social media the ways of influence are many. Far from propaganda being a relic of the old cold war, modern-day social media influence activities routinely feed the news cycle to achieve specific offline actions.

One non-militarised form of propaganda you will be familiar with is politics, where the scramble for your vote is based on influencing your perceptions of a party or individual through staged events and rehearsed monologues that tend to promise a lot and deliver little.

Politicians in office routinely attempt to influence the public into believing self-serving information. From the threat of bushfires or terrorism to the dangerous ineptitude of the opposition party, fear mongering is a core influence enabler that is leveraged continuously. Add social media into the mix and you have all manner of visual content served up in an attempt to win your vote at the next poll.

If politicians are actively and overtly trying to influence your views and voting preferences on social media, and information operations is an accepted military function during times of war, why is it so surprising that the corporate sector has been busy doing exactly the same thing?

Welcome to a new era of crisis communications: the era of influence.

Why influence is key to mission success from battlefield to boardroom

If data is the currency of the future, influence is how it will be traded.

Influence in the era of social media is a peculiar bedfellow for organisations, as the delineation between *individual* and *employee* is greyer than 50 shades of erotic literature.

> 🐦 **Tweet this**
> If data is the currency of the future, influence is how it will be traded #SMROE

The #AllViewsAreMyOwn tag that is littered across social media profiles around the web is a surefire signal that an organisational social media policy is in play — and that the battle between corporate oversight and individual privacy is raging.

Organisations can be held vicariously liable for the social media commentary of their employees during the course of their employment, but the damage caused by rogue social activity after hours is rarely contained to just the individual. With the press always looking for social media profiles, pictures, Facebook posts and tweets to build a story around, organisations can quickly find themselves facing collateral crisis.

Interestingly, the risk doesn't start at the beginning of a crisis; it starts at the moment of organisational recruitment.

The influence equation

Let's toss a coin. Heads: you win an employee with a large social entourage. Tails: you win an employee with a limited digital footprint.

Heads

Your latest star recruit has a social media entourage that rivals that of a B-grade celebrity. Selfies on Instagram, tweeps and fans — their social and online influence is established.

With this recruit comes:

- strong network and brand ambassadorship
- an ability to engage in new markets and networks
- a level of public profile
- a strong understanding of digital and social channels.

Tails

Your latest star recruit had a MySpace account, when they were 14. Their digital footprint is limited to a LinkedIn profile, which has 47 connections but no picture. A quick Google search of their name comes up with some random individual in Uruguay who broke the world record for playing their guitar for four hours while hanging upside down in a tree.

With this recruit comes:

- no online profile or influence
- umm
- well … they tick all the boxes. Qualifications: tick. Experience: tick. Police check: tick.

So call — heads or tails? Heads, you win an employee with influence and a large amount of social media risk. Tails, you win an employee with a large amount of social media risk.

Ahh, you noticed that risk element they share?!

Who do you think is riskier? An employee who knows their way around social media and has used this knowledge to their benefit without scandal (so far); or an employee who is a social media novice, with no social smarts and no understanding of the digital landscape.

From a crisis communications point of view, calling tails is inordinately riskier in the short to medium term, while calling heads presents an accepted, informed level of risk. Both sides of the coin involve risks that can be mitigated, but at the end of the day you're still missing out on the influencer's influence.

Propaganda in your pocket — influence in everyday life

You're never going to look at your loyalty scheme rewards quite the same way after reading this. But the truth is: they're all a con.

Influence activities are, by definition, mostly covert attempts at propaganda. From free flights to vouchers to vacuum cleaners, building brand loyalty is actually about building big data with the aim of influencing your shopping habits, and therefore your spending habits.

Take your grocery shopping rewards as an example. Every time you shop you swipe your loyalty card and earn points, while at the same time giving your purchasing data to the store, which then builds a profile of what kind of customer you are.

From the products you buy most to the 'stage-of-life' shopper you are (think nappies and formula to paleo and dairy free), every time you swipe, you add to the profile your grocery store has of you as a consumer. Of course, that's a profile they don't always keep to themselves.

The odds are firmly stacked in the loyalty scheme's favour. You spend many times the actual fair market cost of a reward while they get your data, your custom and your money. They may have even succeeded in influencing your shopping habits.

Savvy grocery chains and big-store conglomerates then use this information to market to you in tailored 'special offers' via email, app and even old-school letterboxing. This isn't about valuing your custom; it's about creating the *perception* that your custom is valued while influencing your spending habits when you are next in store. As in they want you to *spend more*.

Every time you use your credit or savings card, banks aggregate your data for the same purpose. From the clothes you buy to the wine you drink, if you've paid for these products electronically, your store-level data is painting a consumer profile of you that will be used to influence your future organisational interactions.

The list of consumer-based influence activity doesn't stop there.

The radio channel you tune to for your news updates, the television stations you watch, the magazines you read, the social networks you use — all these sources influence the way you see the world, how you think about certain topics and how you react in defined circumstances.

For crisis communicators, this is a double-edged sword. The big data bonanza aside, the new media propaganda cycle can work decidedly against you during organisational crises; on the other hand, if you are in control of your narrative, you can feed the beast to your benefit.

When strategising crisis messaging, now more than ever, the *how* and *where* are key to successfully influencing perceptions.

Tinker, tailor, soldier … social media spy

Tinfoil hats on! The NSA, DoD, CIA, FBI, KGB and WTF are listening in.

Hands up if you were genuinely surprised by the information leaked by former NSA contractor and now Russian resident Edward Snowden. No? Me neither.

What about Bradley Manning's alleged theft of classified information from the United States military that fueled the WikiLeaks phenomenon. Were you surprised by the content of those revelations?

No? What about that time when Facebook changed their algorithms to manipulate news feeds to create emotional responses? Still not surprised, huh?

If you're on social media, you've freely given away more personal information to the likes of Facebook, Twitter, LinkedIn and Instagram than you give to your bank, employer or sometimes even your spouse.

Social media networks keep more personal data than any other organisations in the world, including governments. Which makes them prime targets for corporate espionage.

Think about it:

- How many of your Facebook friends have you met in real life?

- How many of your LinkedIn connections do you know personally or have you worked with?

- Do you know all the followers you have on Instagram and Twitter?

Now add Google to the equation. How searchable are you?

> 🐦 **Tweet this**
> Social media networks keep more personal data than any other organisations in the world, including governments #SMROE

Unless you've been living in a cave since 2003, I'll wager you've given more than a little thought to the question of how much of your personal data is kept online in the vaults of social networks and search engines around the world.

It's a relevant question, not only from a reputational viewpoint, but also from an OPSEC (operations security) angle. If you're in the military, in intelligence or even a bean counter in a multinational corporation, your digital footprint could make you a target for fraudsters, espionage or identity theft.

The knock-on effects this has on an employer(s) can be catastrophic — if, for example, an individual has done the wrong thing by posting certain pictures, information or geo-tagging locations online.

Crisis communicators and information operations specialists should therefore take particular note of crises arising from individualised sources. When a person is the cause of a crisis, it is no longer enough to attempt to contain the damage relative to any offline outcomes.

Doing an audit of the individual's social media presence and online search results is essential to ensuring there are no other crisis ignition points lurking about ready to surprise you. If your organisation is in a particularly information-sensitive environment, pre-employment screening should include a social media and online audit. At the least, some educational awareness relative to your organisation should be provided to new employees (and existing employees) during induction training.

Another factor to consider is organisation-specific OPSEC requirements: has a crisis compromised the safety and/or security of your organisation and those within it?

It could be as simple as training staff *not* to tweet during building evacuations or lockdown scenarios. Or it could involve requiring staff to lock down their social media accounts and actively vet potential connections.

In considering your risks around social media espionage, do not discount the organisational aspect of blue- or white-collar crime. Leaking corporate secrets via social streams is exceedingly easy to do, both intentionally and unintentionally.

As with your other known organisational risks, social media espionage pertinent to your organisation may need to be included in your crisis communications risk mitigation planning.

Still wearing your tinfoil hat?

Hearts and minds: are you on the communications offensive?

> *So we must be ready to fight in Vietnam, but the ultimate victory will depend upon the hearts and the minds of the people who actually live out there.*

US President Lyndon B. Johnson, 1965

Strategic purpose.

Are you spouting monologues like a dictator trying to retain power? Or are you creating a socially savvy strategic dialogue to engage and influence?

It's an important question to ask, because the outcomes of your communications will vary considerably depending on the impetus behind the *why* of your communication in the first place.

Your organisation may be unconsciously influencing its audience through a sales and marketing mindset. There is, however, significant strategic deviation in the ways influence is exerted in the short and longer term to enable crisis communicators to work their magic.

As a crisis communicator, everything you do should be the result of deliberate strategic intent: you must consistently influence your audience toward the desired outcome one step at a time. More importantly, to ensure your success your crisis communications activities should not be run in isolation of broader corporate communications objectives.

And herein lies the quandary faced by many crisis communicators when dealing with large organisations. While you're hosing down rampant speculation and spot fires at stage left, the marketing department are singing songs of joy and rapture at stage right *after* the grand finale. Cue the final curtain — the show's over.

In the military, influence is most often operationally geared. It has traditionally dealt with the here-and-now of war in each geographical area. Apart from trying to convince the locals to stop shooting at your soldiers, you also have to convince the folks at home — sometimes while in the political crosshairs, dodging rapid fire — that they too should be supporting your efforts.

This is not unlike what happens in boardrooms. While dealing with the crisis here and now may seem like the prudent course of action, you inevitably get caught in the crosshairs of organisational bureaucracy and are left to convince an internal and external audience of the merits of your decisions.

So if crisis communicators — or any communicators — are continually vying with external factions for influence and narrative dominance, why aren't we building military-style influence into our business-as-usual content?

That press release: is it a quick update of the last one you sent out, or have you put some thought into why people should care about whatever it is you're announcing?

That social media post: are you posting for the sake of posting, rather than using your social media networks to prime your audience toward expecting meaningful announcements and definitive calls-to-action?

Those talking points: can they be broken down into 140-character bursts so the media adviser can simultaneously tweet the press conference to break news and control the narrative, or are you taking hours to upload the transcript to the web?

On social media, the weight of *what* you say is always influenced by the weight of *how and where* you say it.

The general topography of communications has changed, meaning you now need to be present in more conversations over the longer term to build credibility before being able to exert influence. Which makes building influence actions into your narrative an essential part of both business as usual and crisis strategies.

> 🐦 **Tweet this**
> On social media, the weight of what you say is always influenced by the weight of how and where you say it #SMROE

In today's communications environment, where narratives that lack substance simply fall by the engagement wayside, there is absolutely no point in communicating unless you are aiming to produce an on- or offline action.

So get on the communications offensive during peacetime (business as usual) and when at war (during crises).

WINNING SOCIAL MEDIA HEARTS AND MINDS

- Know what actions you want to influence within your audience ahead of time, and build influence into your planning for organisational crises and business as usual.

- Prime your communications channels over the long game to ensure your audience is primed for hard calls to action.

- Measure your online impacts. Is the influence you are exerting across different social media networks working? Target your efforts accordingly.

- Look at your organisation's social media data. Is your target audience firmly entrenched in your demographics or are you selling surfboards to Eskimos?

- Develop engaging, authentic content that exerts influence, by consciously steering away from the over-representation of soft content in your communications.

- If you're pushing content to offline channels, how are you measuring any resulting influence outcomes?

If you're not using influence tactics to build your organisation's online profile, how do you expect to be competitive in an influence-infused news media and marketplace?

The men who stare at goats: the power of social media conspiracy theories

'More of this is true than you would believe ...', quoting from the film, *The Men Who Stare at Goats*, but information has long been used as a weapon of war. From the leaflets dropped from hot-air balloons over Prussia in the 1870s to the social media jihadism of today — broadcasting your communications into enemy territory is an integral part of modern warfare.

Misinformation, too, aimed at swaying hearts and minds in conflicts to influence both civilian populations and military combatants, has a long and illustrious history.

A lesser-known military strategy centres on Psi, or parapsychology, the study of paranormal and psychic phenomena. Psi's use in warfare isn't a new phenomenon, but its application on the modern battlefield is noteworthy for socially savvy military information operators.

A short stroll through history reveals tales of psychic spies, spoon-bending agents and KGB superheroes. If you think that all sounds like an episode of *Ripley's Believe it or Not*, read the books for yourself.

In his memoir *The Stargate Chronicles*, Joseph McMoneagle details a career as a psychic spy with the United States Army. Jonathan Margolis's biography *The Secret Life of Uri Geller: CIA Masterspy?* explores Geller's covert work with the Mossad and the CIA. In *Psychic Discoveries Behind the Iron Curtain*, Sheila Ostrander and Lynn Schroeder document extensive research in the field during a journey through Russia, Bulgaria and Czechoslovakia in 1967.

Psi — believe it or not? Well actually, that's exactly the point.

More colloquially referred to by the military as PSYOP (or MISO, for Military Information Support Operations), its purpose is to control perceptions in ways that have direct and physical impacts in an area of operations.

PSYOP + social media = an unparalleled opportunity to tap into the hive-infused, news cycle hyperbole culture of information consumerism.

It's a constant game of digital one-upmanship. In the battlespace this leads to social-micro dominance and mission success. In the boardroom it equates to sales, revenue and market share dominance.

Consider celebrity culture for a moment, arguably the biggest PSYOP run on the civilian population of our time. The likes of Kim Kardashian and Paris Hilton generate obscene incomes from the public perception they have created of themselves. We all know it's a Botox-infused play on the West's predilection for superficial consumerism under the guise of a sponsored façade, but that doesn't make their civilian PSYOP endeavours any less profitable. In fact, their calls-to-action produce very profitable offline actions.

The little-known truth about PSYOP is that social media is primed for channel exploitation — from both the battlefield and boardroom.

The mass media, marketeers and in many cases governments have primed the public to receive multiple short bursts of information that follow distinct narratives. Essentially exploiting the human condition's need to share stories, savvy organisations are simply reverse engineering social media networks for PSYOP purposes.

Another by-product of the social media revolution is content shareability. Far from being critically discreet about what they share, the general population are in it for the LOLs, the awe factor, the weird-but-true and freaky curiosities of life. People are willingly duped into believing conspiracy theories, particularly in audience segments that are already highly mistrustful of government and among whom cultural superstitions are prevalent.

During information vacuums, the news media in particular resort to publishing conspiracy dressed up as journalism to cover the 'no-new-news' truth. As long as people keep consuming this type of content, the cycle will continue.

As a tactic of modern warfare, PSYOP-infused social media content, however implausible, can singlehandedly generate enough doubt to cause actions in the physical domain. Savvy PSYOP planners can create online distraction and feed the news media's insatiable appetite for stories while controlling a very strategic narrative.

You can scuttle your marketplace adversaries' routine and mundane marketing plays with a well-targeted PSYOP. Think, for example, of the

National Australia Bank's cheeky Valentine's Day 'I'm breaking up with you' messages to the other big banks. The campaign produced an offline impact: new customers opened accounts with the bank.

Whether your PYSOP army is staring at goats, bending spoons or producing daring marketing campaigns, the result is a multi-staged, labyrinthine sociological on- and offline offensive. As one tool in the influence operator's kitbag, it can reach far beyond the battlespace or boardroom, tapping into the global social media audience in a Google ranking spectacular that money couldn't buy.

> 🐦 **Tweet this**
> Your audience is looking for a story. So be a storyteller and give them an adventure! #SMROE

Is your organisational or military unit churning out an endless stream of unimaginative press releases? Or are you reading the play for opportunities for maximum, newsjacked audience impact? Whether or not you believe the story itself is true, there is an important lesson that can be learned from the Hollywood movie *The Men Who Stare at Goats*.

Your audience is looking for a story. So be a storyteller and give them an adventure!

A rumour of war: the art of social media counter-public-relations

Do you remember the old game of Chinese whispers (called telephone in the US)? A message is whispered from one person to the next, ear to ear down the line, until the last person declares the message to the group. What is interesting is how often the message has changed, slightly or radically, after a number of retellings.

Rumours of war, whether on the battlefield or in the boardroom, are no different. In fact, with the advent of social media, such rumours can have precise strategic impacts. For example, it's never been easier to divert attention away from an adversary by deploying a slick, targeted social media campaign that captures the news media and fuels social media consumerism into a frenzy of likes, retweets and shares.

> 🐦 **Tweet this**
> It's never been easier to divert attention away from an adversary by deploying a slick, targeted social media campaign #SMROE

Though lacking the wholesale detail of full-blown conspiracy theory, rumour plays a part in creating and directing influence. In fact, the more outlandish the story, the more likely it is to gather social media and news media traction.

Urban legend

What urban legends are you familiar with in your area of operation or marketplace? Are there prevailing cultural superstitions in your geographical area? Is there, for example, a general mistrust of political and religious sentiment? What urban references are associated with your brand? Your organisation? You should be seeing opportunity here.

Fanning existing flames of revolutionary discontent; starting rumours of war; tapping into the hive mentality of social media users, particularly in cultures that are predisposed to communicating and thinking collectively—all are potential PSYOP influence actions that are geographically relevant to local and international narratives.

Well-planned, -targeted and -deployed rumours based on urban legend can quickly overwhelm your adversary's narrative. Quickly outmaneuvering them in order to stay consistently one step ahead becomes a game that those lacking social strategy and tactics won't be able to keep up with.

With armchair generals and smartphone warriors now a fixture in modern conflict, whether on the battlefield or in the boardroom, you need to create your own narratives, weaving the rumour of adversary weakness into your crisis communications.

MY STORY: COMMUNICATIONS CROSSROADS—LIFE OUTSIDE MY COMFORT ZONE

When I imagined where my blogging might take me, I was thinking more along the lines of the beaches of Hawaii, tapping away on my MacBook while gazing out at another tropical sunset. I ticked that off my list in 2012, and since then my blog has taken me on adventures beyond anything I could have imagined.

In late October 2014 I found myself standing at the front of a large auditorium full of military officers representing the 28 nations of NATO at NATO School in the United States. There I was, on one of the world's largest naval bases, delivering a lecture on terrorism and the advent of social media jihad.

A blogger. Lecturing NATO. In person. #Surreal.

At the time I was freshly out of the Australian Public Service, having taken a leap of faith by investing in myself and the blogging profile I'd built up over the previous four years. It wasn't an opportune time to leap, but then when is?

I've always been a firm believer that life opens doors for you, and it's up to you whether you walk through them toward new adventures or you walk on past, back into your comfort zone.

My story is probably unlike most former public servants in that I had an exit strategy up my sleeve. I had an internationally successful blog, a large social media presence and global repute as a thought leader in social media–based military information operations.

I had an exit strategy because at the six-year mark of my career, at the tail end of my transition from operational to corporate work, I'd transferred from the Australian Customs and Border Protection Service to Australia's Defence Materiel Organisation (DMO). Accepting a position as an executive-level strategic communications adviser, I set about the task of remediating a divisional reputation that had been battered by the media and hostile Senate estimates hearings. I hadn't been in the job long before I realised the organisation was stuck in the communications dark ages. Knowing I didn't want to become an organisational relic, gathering taxpayer dust, I saw I needed a future-self exit strategy.

I had a vision of what I could achieve outside of the public service, so I began blogging.

The silver lining of my time in the DMO (and what kept me there longer than I intended) was being able to work with Army, Air Force and, less frequently, Navy service personnel within the Australian Defence Force.

From spinning around the Monegeetta Proving Ground with successive ministers strapped into Bushmaster and Hawkei protected mobility vehicles, to seeing the Mercedes-Benz G Wagons into service at RAAF Base Amberley to working with the Army's Diggerworks team, I found the men and women of the ADF as professional as they were generous with their time in producing great communications content.

The DMO, in contrast, was crisis and issues central, a rich training ground for a crisis communicator. There were the never-ending acquisition and procurement debacles: the soles of parade shoes literally falling off soldiers' feet (while on parade); uniforms ripping while soldiers were fighting the Taliban in Afghanistan — I was never short of a media enquiry to respond to or an issue to back-brief someone on.

But after successive organisational disappointments, refusing to walk past a standard I'd have to accept, I walked out the door and into the life I'd built around my blog.

In the six months that followed, I rode the wave of my blogging success as news spread that I was now working as an international freelancer.

I turned my successful blog into two, co-founding a new company, Info Ops HQ, in the process. From July to December 2014 I travelled across Asia and the United States talking about social media warfare and social media jihad. From Thailand, Singapore, South Korea and Malaysia to Japan, United States and Belgium, my unplanned adventure was a taste of things to come.

I signed this global book deal with Wiley. I joined the professional speaking circuit, delivering keynotes to industry associations and conferences on social media crisis communications and risk management. I co-built a military think tank on information operations with a global client base.

And the best part? I'm working on causes that I'm passionate about, with people who are achieving amazing things, in a positive, inspiring environment.

So, a personal lesson from a crisis communicator who found herself at a corporate crossroads: invest in yourself and navigate your own way to achieving the career goals of your dreams. If you have a vision of a more productive way of working, a more holistic way of living, and you can apply yourself to achieving that vision, *you* can create your next communications career adventure.

Communicators, especially those who have been institutionally exposed to crisis in fast-paced, high-stakes environments, are by nature exceedingly adaptable. We pick our battles carefully, we're incredibly resilient and we always play to win.

Now is an incredible time to be a communicator. Never before in the history of humankind have we had a single universal communications language: social media.

Unlike our forebears, we aren't confined by language, geographical, academic or technological limitations. Communicators are now writing history in the organisations they work for and the communities they belong to. They are also creating their own legacies, spanning generations of family tradition and capturing the stories of the human condition that aren't often told.

You are your own storyteller. You are in control of your own narrative. What will your communications legacy be? Where will your next communications adventure take *you*?

9

Lie to me:
why you can't fool your social media audience

Spinning stories has never been easier, yet separating fact from fiction has never been harder.

What to believe?

Social media audiences are hungry for outrageous conspiracy theories and magic goblins sprinkling fairy dust over the latest OMG, can you believe it's true?! Until a multinational or politician tries to fly a not-so-truthful story past them, at which point shrieks of social outrage can be heard ricocheting around the internet.

Exhausting, isn't it? The truth is (pun intended!) social media audiences are happy to believe that a woman has three breasts but are more sceptical when it comes to the stories around organisational crises.

The crisis communicators waltz on social media is simple: people *want* to believe in aliens, dragons and the Loch Ness Monster, but they are suspicious of a police force that 'accidentally' tweeted porn from their official account.

Truth, it appears, is relative to your audience and the believability factor of a crisis. Unfortunately for crisis communicators, the believability ratio is near impossible to define. Which makes a long waltz with the truth the logical communications choice during an organisational crisis.

IRL (in real life): the human factor

While I've written a lot about the benefits of being social media data and analytics savvy, I can't stress enough how important the human factor is in making robust assessments about your social media communications during a crisis.

To avoid any misunderstanding, the human factor is *YOU*. Data doesn't have practical sensibilities — *you do*. Data doesn't know what is happening in the rest of your organisational world relative to your crisis — *you do*. Data can't tell the difference between your actual audience and the rubber-necking public who have on-boarded simply to delight in the trail of #PRFail carnage you've left in your wake — *you can*.

SOME MORE THINGS THAT SOCIAL MEDIA DATA *CAN'T* HELP YOU WITH

- What to communicate.
- How to ease tensions and remediate the situation.
- How to show leadership, character and organisational conviction.
- Where the boundary between organisational ethics and morality lies.
- How close to, or far across, the lines of industry codes of conduct, legislation or standards of professional practice your crisis is flying you.
- How long a transition to business as usual will take you.

The numbers may give you good indications of how things are tracking, but it's more important to bring your expertise, common sense and situational sensibilities to the crisis communications table. All the social media tools in the world won't help you if you can't communicate effectively IRL.

With myriad data sets available, it's easy for organisations and crisis communicators alike to form an over-reliance on the pretty analytical graphs and quantifiable statistics executives love. However, crisis communicators must always keep in mind that data is only a tool to be used to inform your views. A piece of the social media puzzle; it should never define your strategy or response.

> 🐦 **Tweet this**
> All the social media tools in the world won't help you if you can't communicate effectively IRL #SMROE

Read the data play and use it to inform your decision making, *but* look at the actual crisis situation from a human point of view too. Read the posts and tweets that are causing your social media–based organisational crisis. Follow the troll trail. Dive into the detail. Because while data will inform you broadly, it won't provide you with the rationale required to move your organisation through crisis to recovery.

Social media profiling: far from a game of cyber cops and robbers

Profiling is still a dirty word.

Connotations of ethnic and gender prejudice arise. People are suspicious of anything that has the word 'profiling' attached to it because of some questionable uses and methods of profiling in the past. Fair call.

The truth, though, is that profiling is still used in various forms and ways. From law enforcement to the military to organisational bean counters and from jihadist groups to banks offering home loans, almost every industry and sector profiles its customers, prospective members or threats in some way to manage data and inform decision making.

Social media is no different. Only instead of calling the companies that specialise in it the 'Social Media Network that Profiles your Online Influence', they're called Klout and Kred.

Both Klout and Kred measure an individual's or organisation's social media influence relative to their peers and other social media users. A key takeaway here is that Kloud and Kred measure *only* social and online influence. Which is where, as with most profiling tools, things can come a little unstuck. What about other influencers? You know, the ones that happen *offline*?

Imagine, for example, you are analysing an online antagonist and they have a high Klout score. You may assume that equates to influence, ergo the threat level posed is high. If you simply take that at face value and make some strategic decisions at this point, you're risking being misinformed. By taking a closer look you will find the devil is always in the detail.

So, what might we find if we dig a little deeper into the detail of their accounts?

Perhaps they are legitimately famous. If they're tweeting anti-sentiment about your brand you really are getting the kind of free publicity you don't want. *But* if you find that, for all the social bravado, their account's engagement doesn't match their profile, their followers are mostly off-shore, and are not aligned with their professed expertise or market presence, you may find they've gamed the system to increase their scores.

Klout and Kred both claim their algorithms detect this type of behaviour and eliminate it from aggregate scores. Well — ask the code monkeys who continuously game Google — there are always ways to adapt to changes in algorithmic behaviour and game the system. This can be easily achieved after a quick visit to online stores where you can buy engagement and followers off the rack at places like fiver.com or freelancer.com, for example.

In contrast, someone with a low Klout score may turn out to be a bigger threat than you first thought. Just because they don't have a Twitter account, aren't on LinkedIn and don't blog, don't underestimate their influence.

There are still many baby-boomer CEOs out there who don't give a toss about social media. They've made their mark and on their journey to retirement they hardly *need* social media to assist their careers, particularly when they can just pay someone to run an organisational account that achieves much the same objectives.

> 🐦 **Tweet this**
> Just because they don't have a Twitter account, aren't on LinkedIn and don't blog, don't underestimate their influence #SMROE

Many people don't want or need the social media entourage we have been talking about, so making judgements on risk based on low Klout scores is unreliable. The same CEO who is not personally enthusiastic about social media may still be able to pick up the phone and have a conversation with a journalist that leads to front-page news on- and offline.

You just don't know who you're talking to on social media.

For all the social profiling available, you still have no idea who is in that person's network and what resources they may have in play that *could* cause you organisational crisis.

For large organisations in particular, the tendency to equate fear with following can be quite profound.

🐦 **Tweet this**
Take the time to look beyond the surface to really understand the social media risk you're facing #SMROE

The lesson? Don't judge a risk or a person based on their social appearances. And don't be automatically impressed by large social entourages and technologically tweaked appearances.

Take the time to look beyond the surface to really understand the social media risk you're facing.

Life in the hive: global social activism and why you should take note

The hive mentality often surrounding social media crises is not dissimilar to a nest of angry bees. The queen bee is the main instigator, whether in the role of antagonist or hero, and her worker bees swarm around her to protect and defend her at all costs.

Urban Dictionary defines the hive mind as:

> when two or more people come to the same thought at the same time because of the same circumstances but do not know each other beforehand (i.e. it cannot be an inside joke). This usually happens on internet message boards, and is especially noticeable when the thought reached is not a meme. The name is reflective of insects who act in unison with their hive (or nest) mates.

Social media users behave in much the same way as a nest of upset bees during online outrage and episodes of social mutiny. Such is the momentum created by an issue that like minds flock to the hive to defend and protect.

It is well worth investing time in seeking to understand the psychology of social media user behaviour in the event of crises. Understanding what is driving your audience's reaction and how their swarm response is forming (such as by natural causal attraction or deliberate troll invitation), you are better situated to make decisions on which tactics to employ to remediate the situation.

If we consider the hive mentality and social media audience anarchy during the Arab Spring, there are key lessons crisis communicators can learn to inform their strategy, planning and tactics:

- Online events can move offline at a rapid pace.

- Social media can fuel outrage to extraordinary levels.

- Social media can cause incidents and events to continue over long periods of time.

More importantly, crisis communicators with social anarchy on their hands need to realise that they have lost their strategic position as narrator in perhaps their own or a broader story.

There will come a point during social media anarchy when the social hive will start writing your narrative for you.

You may not like how that narrative is developing, but throwing all your resources into operational influence here will have little if any effect. You simply cannot out-influence a hive mentality of large numbers of social media users.

The best strategy at this point is quite literally to retreat and not be drawn into the confrontation that the hive so clearly wants you to be part of. Say your piece and then say nothing. Social anarchy will rage on with or without you, so disengage and instead focus your efforts ahead of the hive, for the time when your voice will be heard again.

Social anarchy will inevitably run out of steam, at which point you can strategically help your audience to move past the events of the past few hours or days by remaining authentic in your engagements and helpful in the information you provide.

Regardless of fault, steer clear of the need to lay blame or defend your organisation over the longer term — it's not necessary. Accepting that you can't always control the narrative, whether you are in the right or wrong, and moving past the incident is always the better approach.

Focusing your crisis communications resources on organisational survival is much more important than giving air time to audiences that never genuinely cared for you in the first place.

MY STORY: LIE TO ME

Skills I picked up in former jobs have proved exceedingly handy in my work as a social media crisis communicator and military information operations adviser.

I choose not to use the tag 'profiler' because I don't think it fits. I'm both more diverse and occupationally less of an expert than the Hollywood connotation of the title suggests. Nevertheless, I can confirm I have been trained in behavioural and analytical profiling.

During my early days as a private investigator, I was mentored by a former Victorian Police detective. Bob (not his real name) has one of the sharpest minds I've ever encountered. He could read a person — face, body and language — and if during an interview that person started to spin a yarn, within minutes Bob would be calling them out on their story, one lie at a time.

Bob taught me a hell of a lot, from how to read body language, to the way my own demeanour and appearance influenced the interview, to vocal inflections, to how to spot clues of deceit in what people said or didn't say. I was incredibly lucky to have learned my trade from such a skilled professional.

Fast forward to my Customs and Border Protection days at Melbourne International Airport and I was again working the deception detection beat. Only instead of insurance frauds, employees on the take and arsonists, I was up against hardened criminals, drug traffickers and terrorists.

The change of pace was intense. The stakes were higher: instead of protecting corporate bank balances, I was protecting the community from people intent on causing harm.

Often when I recount this time in my life to people, they struggle with the idea that I might apply these skills outside of the law enforcement arena. They assume I'm still in the zone and am digesting and analysing their every micro expression, their every word.

Perhaps that's because we're a secretive fraternity out of operational necessity, or perhaps it's a simple case of lack of a narrative to debunk the prevailing perceptions.

While I do have a heightened sense of situational awareness, it's also true to say that I don't use my Spidey senses unless someone or a situation gives me good reason to. Living my private and professional life through the acuity of an operational lens isn't living – it's paranoia. It's just a tool of the trade: used when it's situationally required.

So from private investigator to Customs and Border Protection officer to crisis communicator and military information operations adviser, here are some of the ways I've used this skill set in social media settings, with tips and tricks you can perhaps apply in your own context.

As a strategic communications adviser and crisis communicator:

- Matching photos to presentations, news articles and promotional material for the Australian Army's Diggerworks unit might seem like a pretty mundane task. Pick the most impressive picture, right? Wrong. The picture chosen has to match your message. Stick a camera in front of someone and their instinctive reaction is to smile – even in a war zone. When the promotional content being developed for on- and offline use has accompanying text of serious intent alongside a picture of a soldier smiling like a

Cheshire cat, the end communications product is off target. As a general rule, soldiers at war shouldn't look overly happy to be in the sandpit going about the business of killing the enemy.

- Ministers of Defence and their ministry counterparts love a good photo opportunity, particularly if they can shake someone's hand, sign some paper and stand in front of some eye-catching hardware like a tank, plane or ship. Officers and soldiers are usually not so impressed by the spectacle, however. Even less so if they have to participate in the ministerial photo opportunity. While the Minister might be beaming in each photograph, editing becomes a process of elimination when the faces of the assembled entourage tell a different story.

As a military information operations adviser I look at photographs and video footage through the eyes of an intelligence analyst seeking to verify an information source:

- While terrorist still and video propaganda imagery often purports to be taken in situ, small details may indicate the image is being recycled from previous conflicts, sometimes of altogether unrelated events that occurred years apart.

- Using still and video imagery on social media as a weapon of war has become routine for social media jihadists and jihadi brides. The pictures, videos and messages they post tell a story far beyond the words used. The news media tend only to scratch the surface of the psychological and ideological narrative revealed in the imagery presented for public consumption.

If you are interested in learning these types of skills to apply to the context of crisis communications, social media or military information operations, I highly recommend Dr Paul Ekman's books and online training products.[1]

---

1. http://nicolematejic.com/my-village-of-support/recommended-reading

10

Lessons from an inferno:
how to be a #SocialFirefighter®

So you want to be a #SocialFirefighter®?

Perhaps you're already a crisis communicator looking for ways to manage social media crisis; perhaps you're a student looking for a challenging career away from the press release production line; or perhaps you're a military information operations specialist seeking new ways to reverse engineer social media for influence activities.

When I guest lecture at universities, one of the most common questions I'm asked by students doing a single semester on crisis communications in a three- or four-year degree is, 'Where do I learn these skills?'

It's a fair question. They recognise that a semester spent with your head in a textbook isn't going to equip you with real-life experiences from which your judgement, strategic and critical thinking skills are developed.

My answer is always the same: You can read about crisis communications in books and blogs; you can watch videos and listen to podcasts — these are all great sources of information, and building your theoretical knowledge in this area is very worthwhile. But at some point, you're going to have to put skin in the game and dive into a role that gives you the opportunity to be mentored by someone experienced in dealing with organisational crises.

I have been fortunate to have been mentored by a range of experienced leaders who were exceptionally good at managing organisational crises and communications simultaneously.

I have also been fortunate to have observed incompetent leaders who have caused crises or have bungled one crisis after another in short order. I say 'fortunate' because each and every time I've encountered people who have failed because of their actions or inactions, I've taken the view that I just received a valuable free lesson in what not to do and how not to behave.

Crisis communicators are built largely from experience. In this book I've recounted several real-life stories from my career to pass on some of that experience to you contextually.

So if crisis communications is your box and dice, where do you find rich experiential training grounds?

- *Crisis communications consultancies.* Often an adjunct of larger communications agencies, these organisations have a diverse client base that presents interns and graduates with a broad range of crisis-related experiences.

- *Offices of government and political parties.* There is nothing quite like the mechanics of government to breed crises. While some ministers and senators are squeaky clean, others have more skeletons in their closet than Imelda Marcos has shoes.

- *Large government communications and public relations teams.* Bureaucracy by nature breeds issues and crises, and the bigger the department the larger the risk. Spending some time in the public service in a department that piques your interest (see my thoughts on building a specialisation below) are proven training grounds with more twists and turns than a yoga lesson.

- *Large multinationals such as banks, mining companies and retailers.* That they are less prone to scandal is often due to the fact that they plan for risk much better than most organisations. Embedding yourself in a corporate communications role in these types of organisations will give you a breadth of experience that is holistically geared.

This list is by no means exhaustive, but it gives you some good starting points when considering your next job-change or planning your career trajectory. The key is to look for environments that will provide you with rich crisis and issues training grounds.

The niche

You can be a crisis communicator generalist or, like me, you can develop a niche or two to specialise in. I specialise in social media and military information operations; you can build your own niche out of your broader experiences, knowledge and qualifications. Other niche crisis communicators I personally know and work with specialise in the aviation sector, the political arena, fast-moving consumer goods, change management, corporate affairs, law and industrial relations.

Marrying up your own interests, experience or pre-existing skill set with your crisis communications skills can be very lucrative. In some contexts a depth of expertise in the subject matter is essential to a communicator's ability to communicate authentically and provide professional advice.

The social smoke detector

In our homes and workplaces, smoke detectors are essential early warning indicators to alert us to a possible fire. In a social media crisis communications context, are you installing early warning indicators and, if so, are you installing them in places most likely to ignite organisationally?

There are key elements of social media crisis that send up red flags to warn you of impending social anarchy. Sadly, most of these flags are missed because either people aren't trained to identify them or a means of identification doesn't exist in the first place.

Social media risk, as discussed in part II, is inextricably linked to the business your organisation is in. There should be no surprises here: that if your organisation runs public transport, for example, a train derailment should top your list of possible organisational risks.

But the smaller elements of risk that can just as easily ignite into full-blown social media #PRFails are often harder to spot. These indicators are tied to the behaviours of your regular social media audience and, during times of impending crisis, the social media population at large.

Just as in real life, the emotions of frustration, anger, hate, happiness and grief drive the way people interact with others. Feelings such as injustice, inequality, bias and discrimination also play a role in human interactions.

Why people express their feelings and emotions on social media is no different from why they express them in real life, only the conduit of expression of those emotions can become any of your organisational social media channels.

Here are some of the types of social media user behaviours that should send up red flags for crisis communicators.

YOU CAN SMELL SMOKE BEFORE YOU SEE FIRE

- Use of profanity in posts, mentions or chatter as a prelude to organisationally directed anger.

- Sharing your content with overtures of undirected anti-sentiment (that is, just because they can, rather than because they had a bad experience with your product or service).

- Continually (habitually) posting on your Facebook wall, tweeting you or otherwise making attempts at online provocation.

- Threats of violence — toward the product, service or organisational personnel.

- The airing of grievances (resolved or unresolved).

- Use of words and statements that indicate a potential for self-harm or intent to harm others.

- Organisational inclusion in attempts at hashtag drama, such as #PRFail, #CrisisComms, #FAIL and #WorstEver (this list isn't exhaustive).

Subjective vs objective

When considering the content and framing of anti-sentiment on social media, you need to look beyond what is being said to discover, within your organisation, if the allegations have any merit.

Posts that are subjective in nature are often highly emotive and speculative and based on personal perception. Posts that are objective in nature are more likely to be based on verifiable evidence, such as a product failure or bad customer experience.

It is important to recognise that perception plays a large role in both your assessment of the information at hand and the way the information has been framed for your consumption.

Regardless, any social interactions that provide objective views should be at least investigated cursorily to determine the level of organisational risk. Savvy communicators can often engage with such interactions and influence a positive outcome. Repeated product failures or poor experiences can start to build a picture of broader organisational liability. Consumer posts to your social media streams may be the way you learn of a product failure, for example.

The litmus test that social media crisis communicators should use to decide if a lone post or tweet has the impetus to start something more sinister is the prevailing audience sentiment in your social media networks.

In isolation, such social media interactions mean little, but when they are part of a broader wave of anti-sentiment, whether that is deliberate or coincidental, the way in which social media networks curate chatter begins to work against you.

From top topical tweets to Facebook posts that spread through timelines, the algorithms in play mean there is a very real risk of isolated instances gaining traction.

Kit up: the tools and skills you need to fight social media fires

To fight social media fires, of course you need to be on social media. You need to be familiar with the same tools, apps, channels and platforms as your audience. You need to know your way around the back-end analytics functions, scheduled posting cycles and retweeting bots. You need to know your hashtags from your Instagrams and your posts from your hangouts.

> 🐦 **Tweet this**
> To fight social media fires, you need to be familiar with the same tools, apps, channels and platforms as your audience #SMROE

From scheduled posts to data and analytics to measurement and monitoring tools, here are my top picks for creating your own social media crisis communicator's kit[1]:

- Hootsuite — a social media management system that has an inbuilt analytics function.

- uberVU — Hootsuite's premium audience sentiment analysis tool, providing instant social insights.

- RepKnight — an open source monitoring platform that produces both sentiment and geographical analysis in real time across all major social media channels.

- TweetReach (also TweetReach Pro) — provides detailed analysis of the impact of a single tweet. Real-time Twitter, Instagram and Tumblr analytics are available in the pro version.

- Mention (app) — a real-time media monitoring tool that also captures social media posts and blog mentions.

- Google Analytics — provides website traffic and source information; handy for crisis communicators to see the conversion rates between social media networks and the web, and vice versa.

You should also make yourself intricately familiar with the inbuilt analytics functions of the social networks your clients use, such as Facebook insights and Twitter and LinkedIn analytics.

On an enterprise level, there are products available that do all this and more for you on the one dashboard — if your client or organisation uses Salesforce, for example, you need to be conversant with the social media customer relationship management and social media tools of that platform.

---

1. http://nicolematejic.com/my-village-of-support/my-social-toolbox

Regardless of the technology your clients may have in play (which you should be conversant with), you still need the old-school ability to do your own legwork during a crisis.

Build a newsroom

Creating news, rather than simply being the subject of it, can be a viable option for many organisations. Effectively cutting out journalists and the news media overlay on your story is a savvy move during times of crisis.

Building a newsroom also provides your online audience with a single point of resource for comment, video, links and transcripts. Making it easy for people to find your narrative is a good way to exert influence.

From a social media perspective, using your channels to broadcast from your personal newsroom is relatively simple. Once you have your content live within your web-based newsroom, you're all set. While the content production overheads can be higher and more resource intensive at the outset, particularly if you want to produce or stream content of high quality, the benefits far outweigh the drawbacks.

> **Tweet this**
> Making it easy for people to find your narrative is a good way to exert influence #SMROE

From a crisis communicator's perspective, organisations that have a newsroom tend to be more media savvy, making the art of communicating during a crisis less complex, as navigating the news media cycle or tapping journalist contacts is cut from the equation.

It also acts as a strong driver for your narrative to be validated as the source of information; this can be critically important in high-stakes crises where speculation occurs during information vacuums. Being the authoritative source of information, and broadcasting that from your own newsroom into your social media networks, is an extremely powerful organisational resource.

Breaking bad: the art of selling your own scandal

Scandal sells news, so how do you navigate out of a crisis when the press is camped outside your office?

Fair warning: the strategy of breaking your own bad news is a hard sell to most organisational decision makers. Many live in the hope that no one will find out about their organisational crisis, or if they do, it won't be a slow news day and they'll be no more than a blip in the online news deluge.

Resistance to this crisis strategy is based on fear, which is a catalyst for the fight-or-flight response (discussed in part II). In the context of crisis communications, this means while some decision makers want to go in, guns blazing, others will already be halfway out the door in retreat.

The fear factor around breaking your own bad news is simple to understand: there is anxiety around losing control over the situation, creating the perception of organisational or personal weakness, and most of all, a fear of secrets being found out.

As a crisis communicator, you're not in the business of passing judgement on the situations that cross your path to remediate. You're in the business of fixing problems, so it's incredibly important to compartmentalise any bias or personal sentiment you have about the situation. If you can't, you should seriously reconsider if you are the best person to act on your client's or organisation's behalf.

Internal crisis communications comes first

When preparing to break organisational bad news, carefully consider your audiences, the most important of which is your internal audience.

They deserve to hear the news first, either in person or via a personal communiqué from a suitably senior organisational leader. This is incredibly important, not only because it's the right thing to do, but also because your internal workforce are the people who will be impacted most by organisational scandal. Morale dives, attrition rises and tempers fray at a time when you need them to remain focused on the 'what next'.

Don't give your internal workforce a reason to dislike you as much as you expect your external audience to. You have the opportunity to trust them with your bad news first, which in return gives them the opportunity to support the organisation as it moves through the stages of crisis remediation.

By telling them first you have the ability to confine their reactions to a specific place and time. This is critical as the time delay between internal and external communications can be very short. Controlling the duration of internal outrage as you move from your organisational mea culpa to 'what comes next' is essential for winning organisational support.

What you don't want is for an outraged internal workforce to take to the social media airwaves after first hearing about your scandal on the nightly news. Or worse, disgruntled employees giving the media tip-offs that will scuttle your plans to break your own bad news first.

Depending on the specific organisational crisis, this could mean:

- locking down organisational social media access to all but the communications leadership team
- segregating employees in locations away from their usual workplace
- specifically requesting social media silence until after you've had the opportunity to break your bad news
- having counsellors and pastoral care on site ready to assist employees who feel emotionally overwhelmed by the situation.

If you're in government or the military, breaking your own bad news often comes with approval strings attached. Don't leave your Minister or Chief of Service to find out about your bad news from an adviser or, worse, the media. They are part of your internal audience; communicate with them on the scandal *early* and often.

The public mea culpa

Breaking the news of your own scandal is all about controlling your own narrative. Being on the front foot gives you the opportunity to shape and define the narrative without appearing adversarial or reactive. It builds public confidence, portrays strong accountability in leadership, and makes it harder for the media and the general public to sustain high levels of anger with you or your organisation.

But an authentic mea culpa works only when built on foundations of honesty and transparency. Forget about selling a spin campaign and making nonsensical bureaucratic statements; break your own bad news simply, concisely and simultaneously across all on- and offline channels.

Call a press conference, have your communications team tweet it live, upload the video to YouTube quickly and be ready to take questions from the media. These are all things you can prepare for before breaking your news, allowing the focus of your resourcing to be on the questions that will follow.

> 🐦 **Tweet this**
> Breaking the news of your own scandal is all about controlling your own narrative #SMROE

The media

The news media are in the business of asking questions. More often than not they already know, or have some idea about, the answers to these questions, so don't run the risk of spinning a yarn. Their social media influence is cumulatively much bigger than yours (unless you are that media empire!) so avoid taking them for granted.

Controlling your own narrative puts you in the driver's seat of your media interactions: you choose who to speak to, when to speak to them and how to publish. Use this to your advantage. If there are media outlets you have built positive relationships with in the past, offer them an exclusive story. Leverage their collective on- and offline power to make sure your message is heard in the way *you* want it to be heard. Serve them content that is ready for upload with a click-play mentality. Make it easy for them to reproduce your quality content, and by default promote your narrative.

If time allows, this approach has its merits, particularly when preparation time is paramount. However, in the race for rating success or the need to break the news quickly yourself, don't discount the power that becoming the newsroom can have for your brand and organisational identity.

Avoid, at all costs, attempts to shut the news media out of the equation. It leads them to suspect that there is more to your story than you are admitting and if there is scandal to be had, the media will rummage through your corporate closet looking for more skeletons. If they can't find any, they may even use creative licence on your legacy.

> 🐦 **Tweet this**
> Avoid, at all costs, attempts to shut the news media out of the
> equation #SMROE

Crisis over: getting back to business as usual

'Great! It's over! Now we can go back to selling stuff!' said the CEO who had only hours earlier asked me to turn off the internet. Apology issued, he thought he was now home free.

'No,' I replied, '…not unless you'd like your social media audience to lynch you first.'

He wasn't the first CEO to make the misguided assumption that once you've dealt with a social media crisis on your terms, everyone else will just get over it too.

They won't. And they won't like you rushing them to 'get past it' either.

The delicate tango that is moving from crisis to business as usual requires that your audience lead and you follow in step with them. Try to move past them and you'll collide again; try to back away and the distance becomes awkward. Best to stay nice and close, but let them lead a little. Engage in some banter. Smile a lot.

When your social audience is still living through the crisis and your response, you can see this in their interactions, the comments they make, the sentiment they spread and share. They still show great interest in the crisis and how you're managing it. Social media interaction levels are high.

When your social audience has moved past the crisis, their engagement around the crisis wanes, and those who do engage appear more sympathetic. They've lost interest.

Don't make the mistake of assuming that since you've danced a technically perfect tango you'll get a high score from the judges, aka your social media audience. They've not entirely forgiven you for stepping on their feet, nor have they forgotten. They've just moved past it—for the time being. A misstep on your part and you're back to following their lead.

The biggest challenge faced by crisis communicators dealing with a social media crisis is the organisation's desire to speed up the recovery process. When their bottom line takes a hit as sales dive or shareholders sell their stocks, the CEO's desire to get back to 'selling stuff' is understandable. This doesn't mean you should be driven by the same motivations as they are. In fact, unless you're angling for repeat business (which I'm not recommending), how long you tango for depends on how long your social media audience's memory is. And provided you don't do anything in the interim to provoke them.

> 🐦 **Tweet this**
> How long you tango for depends on how long your social media audience's memory is #SMROE

Convincing the CEO to back off sales for a period and concentrate on rebuilding social trust is best achieved by using their own communication currency — that is, what matters most to them.

The key to moving from social media crisis to remediation to business as usual is to ease into that last tango by taking the lead again, with a little soft content to test the waters. An organisational human-interest story, a strategic look behind the scenes.

Go in hard or go in too early and you miss out on the biggest opportunity a crisis presents: to show your audience and the public that have tuned in that *you have heard them.*

Crisis in command

What happens when your CEO or leadership team is the cause of your crisis or scandal? Who will step up to take the organisational communications lead as they fight for their career or fall on their sword?

An absence or failure in leadership is one scenario that organisations routinely *don't* plan for. But having a second, third and even fourth alternative leader identified is essential not only for succession planning, but also for a tiered response to corporate communications during a crisis.

As a general rule, if your CEO or a member of the leadership team is the cause of the crisis, they need to be sequestered away from the organisation as quickly as possible.

This doesn't necessarily mean sacking them. You are a crisis communicator, not a human resources guru. it means you need to ensure that the communications risks surrounding the individual are contained:

- They shouldn't be carrying on as if nothing has happened.
- They shouldn't be active on social media.
- They shouldn't be dealing with the media.

It's a job in crisis containment.

Sounds harsh, but are you willing to bring down an entire organisation for the sake of a single individual? This may be an outcome for an owner-operated business, but for everyone else there are shareholders, ministers, boards, generals and government to answer to.

The best way to manage a crisis around someone is to manage *them* first.

Your organisational actions will speak louder than your organisational words. Make them count. Let natural justice prevail, be compassionate and considerate, but be judicious in the protection of your organisational interests.

🐦 **Tweet this**
The best way to manage a crisis around someone is to manage them first #SMROE

Throwing people under the corporate bus or feeding them to the media sharks is *not* a narrative that your audience wants to read. You're not in the business of selling salacious news. Avoid the corporate temptation to leverage the scandal to your own benefit. It puts you on a collision course with disaster: it's unprofessional, it screams scapegoat and it damages your reputation.

Don't take the focus away from *their* individual scandal and make it yours. However you try to spin it, publically treating people badly via post, tweet or press release will just reflect badly on *your* organisation. The less said organisationally the better. Every story has two sides, and not everyone plays fair.

MY STORY: 'YOU FOUND THAT OUT ... ON A BLOG?'

Back in 2008 during my first foray into using social media for OSINT, I was trawling through my daily batch of Google Alerts. The algorithm at the time wasn't very precise and I had more misses than I had hits.

My then boss had given me some free rein to test my theory, to see if I could come up with any information of value to the intelligence unit in which I was working. While there is no doubt Customs and Border Protection have long since moved on from the days of my rudimentary cyber rummaging adventures, their willingness to explore new ways of detecting border-related crime was even then entirely progressive.

Innovative workplace culture aside, it's safe to say everyone (me included) was surprised when I hit the Google Alerts jackpot. Surprised because instead of catching a little fish, I hooked a whopper.

Using the old Babelfish online translator to take the blog from its language of origin to English, I began to comprehend that I had discovered a nefarious group of individuals who were planning a trip to Australia. Ever helpful in the information they published on their blog, these not so clever criminals had even listed their itinerary and the places they would be visiting on their trip.

Boss: You found that where?

Me: On a blog.

Boss: And it cross-matches with other information we have?

Me: Yep.

Boss: ☺ Nice work.

Cue multi-agency border interventions. Community protected. Case closed. New information-gathering theory: proven.

As I shared my newly minted methodology with other intelligence analysts, I began to appreciate that I was standing on the edge of a precipice, that the cyber information environment was about to take a quantum leap, not just for law enforcement and intelligence personnel, but for everyone – individuals and organisations alike.

It's a journey I'm still on today.

Crazy ideas. Sometimes they happen at the coalface. Where the crisis waiting in the wings is mitigated before it gets to the echelons of CEOs, boards and crisis communicators. But why wait for a crisis to arise? Is your organisation capturing information on near misses? What story is that aggregate of internal information telling you?

If aggregates of data are all singing the same binary tune, you may have just discovered a new way to avert crisis in your organisation.

11

The social grapevine:
why seeing shouldn't always be believing on social media

Do you trust what you read on social media?

Think back to when Facebook and Twitter first hit our desktops. In those first few years of social networking, this kind of information dissemination and consumption was a new thing. We were naturally suspicious of things we read online. The internet was still in its relative infancy. Even Wikipedia was not considered dependable. We still relied on print news, radio and television as our primary sources of information.

Fast forward over a decade to today. I'm going to guess that you're now far more amenable to trusting the information and news you consume via online and social sources. In fact, you may even treat Wikipedia as an authoritative source.

How times change! But what if as a result of this change we've lost the ability to think critically and objectively about the news, information, images and video served up to us?

This question presents crisis communicators, particularly those entrenched in the social media and information operations space, with some significant challenges. They need not only to contend with the deliberate misreporting that is prevalent in a click-bait culture of selling news, but also to critically question the information and content they are served up with when managing organisational crisis.

Regardless of the source of the information, whether internal or external, now more than ever crisis communications must be savvy to the ways of information duplicity and recycling to avoid igniting secondary crises.

Information verification

Someone hands you a picture in the midst of your organisational crisis. They say they got it from someone else, who remembers it being taken on a worksite a while ago. It fits the bill. It's what you've been looking for to add to your crisis social media content. You already have some words in mind that will match it perfectly.

This is the point where you should STOP. Put the picture down and ask the person who so kindly brought it to your attention to verify its origins — that is, confirm its authenticity, 110 per cent.

You should be asking questions such as these:

- If it came from a worksite, have we used this picture before?
- Who was the photographer?
- Exactly when was this photograph taken?
- And where is the exact location depicted?

Because if you don't have a confident recollection of the photo or the ability to validate it yourself, you should be asking yourself some other questions:

- Is this even our worksite?
- What is the context of the photograph?
- Why was it taken in the first place?
- If the image depicts people (presumably employees), do you have their consent to use their image? (Note: just because an employee is *an employee* doesn't give you the automatic right to use their image.)
- Has this image been used by the organisation before?
- In what context?

Just as you can't simply take pictures of your employees and post them to social media without their consent, you can't simply reuse and re-spin images with different meanings to suit new, crisis-led purposes. Your social media audience will spot the reused image and will call you on it.

Cue crisis number 2: looking extra silly because you've just portrayed your organisation as having little regard for attention to detail or, worse, trying to pass off an old image as a new one.

Sex, lies and rocket launchers

One of the most intriguing developments in social media warfare is the recycling of imagery from one conflict to another.

For example, we've seen evidence indicating that images used in relation to the conflicts in the Ukraine, Iraq and Syria had their true origins in Chechnya some years prior. Even the tragic downing of Malaysia Airlines flight 17 over the Ukraine threw up instances of bogus imagery used to influence social media.

Crisis communicators, military or civilian, can easily be caught in this web of deceit, knowingly or perhaps unknowingly—although I'd argue that if you don't validate the authenticity of the imagery you use, then there is a degree of negligence attached to your decision making. Have you ever considered why you don't normally see a news outlet reuse the same image in relation to contrasting narratives.

Remember the adage 'A picture is worth a thousand words'? When you publish an image with a headline and story, or even just a tweet to accompany it, you frame the image. It may be a photo of a woman watching children in a busy playground, but if the headline reads 'Anti-vaccination crusading mother puts other children at risk', the photo is forever linked to that story. Once published in that context, you can't take those connotations and the perceptions you've created back.

Which makes verifying the origins of your imagery exceptionally important, not only in times of crisis but at any point in your social media content strategy.

It's also worth noting that for the same reasons, the use of stock imagery can be problematic (and insincere).

Hijacked! Coincidence? Unlikely

When reading about the latest corporate Twitter account to be hacked, do you ever wonder whether it might have more to do with a targeted organisational social media attack than a poor password and bad luck?

Consider this: as the currency of influence has increased over the past few years, so too has the damage a social media hacker can inflict. We've already seen instances of share market stock price falls, civil unrest following hacked Twitter streams, well-timed leaks of information via hacking, and the financial impacts these can have on an organisation.

> 🐦 **Tweet this**
> Crisis communicators now need to keep firmly in their remediation scope a view of organisational threats and hacker end games #SMROE

For social media crisis communicators, this means a change in perspective when managing crises triggered by hacking. It is no longer enough simply to pick up the pieces of a shattered Twitter stream after a hacker's spree. Crisis communicators now need to keep firmly in their remediation scope a view of organisational threats and hacker end games.

TYPICAL HACKING THREATS BASED ON AN OPPORTUNISTIC APPROACH TO ORGANISATIONAL RISK

- Stock market activities, such as the scheduled or forecasted release of Initial Public Offerings (IPOs) or floats.

- New product launches, announced or unannounced (don't discount the trusted insider leaking information out of the organisation).

- Major announcements, such as annual reports, leadership changes and sales figure updates.

The hacker's end game can be motivated by:

- *government policy*. This could include sanctions against a particular country, comments made in regard to a specific group of people or a perceived injustice against minority groups.

- *military activities*. Simply being present in another geographic region is often enough to provoke cyber conflict, as is any publicised mistreatment of prisoners of war or combat actions.

- *activism*, from animal rights to environmental issues and the treatment of refugees. Online activists can target organisations based on real or perceived affiliations with causes they support or are opposed to.

Crisis communicators must also consider the timing of instances of organisational hacking as it may open avenues of causal investigation (particularly in areas of information security). When you understand that hacking is less opportunistic, particularly toward large organisations, governments and militaries, and that targets are selected for particular reasons to achieve particular outcomes, the way to plan for such crises changes.

Crisis communicators should therefore plan not only for the risk of the hack itself, but also around the organisational risks that predispose the organisation to hacking in the first place.

Newsjacking

Taking what's happening in the news and making a story out of it with commentary relevant to your niche is one of the savviest ways to get traction on social media. It's the modern equivalent of getting on your soapbox, or jumping on that bandwagon.

While building influence via newsjacking is possible, at some point on that trajectory your audience will start to wonder what it is about your contribution that is original. What else do you offer? Where is the value in their interaction with you, apart from some LOLs or an alignment of views?

Your commentary may be authentic and engaging, but there are many pop culture newsjacker identities out there, and at some point they start to suffer from a lack of the diversification that a dynamic social media and online presence requires.

Existing in a single dimension online can mean a very limited digital lifespan because after the shock-jock allure has begun to wear off, you lack a quality of audience connection that drives meaningful engagement. The type of engagement that makes people want to do business with you and buy your products.

After all, you're just jumping on the latest bandwagon. Where is the authentic *you* in the equation? Where is the driver that will convert readers to sales, clients or raving fans?

For individuals and organisations, taking a blasé approach to newsjacking can be fraught with near misses and epic fails. If you're going to do it, you need to be able to pull it off exceptionally well, and (unless you're in the business of newsjacking) it shouldn't be a regular feature in your content cycle.

Newsjacking your way *into* crisis is easy. Trying to newsjack your way out of one by latching onto another story is a diversionary tactic that social media audiences will spot at 10 tweets. It's disingenuous.

So where does newsjacking fit into the crisis communications equation?

Quite simply, it doesn't. It is one part of your social media content equation. The lesson in newsjacking for crisis communicators is to litmus test organisational forays at 'jumping on the bandwagon' against the sentiments of your audience. If newsjacking is the cause of organisational crisis or a near miss, what triggered the audience backlash? And how can you ensure that this doesn't occur again?

Journalism: now just a profession that you used to know

I am not alone in my dismay at the state of professional journalism around the world. I have an experientially and occupationally suspicious view of the news media, but the problem is less to do with the journalists themselves and more to do with the news companies they work for.

The sad truth is that the priority of selling ad space, banners, rotating gifs and advertorials on news websites compromises journalists' ability to practise their craft conscientiously. Perhaps if the multinational corporations that feed us our news were geared less toward profit and more toward the fundamental principles of journalism we might see a change in the way stories are told, framed and sold under click-bait headlines. Until then, it's up to citizen journalists, bloggers and social commentators to fight the good information fight.

For crisis communicators this means that the news media aren't necessarily your biggest allies in communicating your way out of a crisis. While they may have the social media numbers and web traffic stats, the impact of a news media approach will depend largely on the individual publication's influence on your particular audience. And news websites, just like newspapers before them, have very distinct audiences.

This makes knowing your audience and having your own newsroom particularly important.

If your organisational audience demographic is geared toward the consumption of information via industry blogs and social commentators, then that's where you need to aim your remediation efforts. Not only are those bloggers and commentators trusted, but they are also influencers in their areas of expertise.

Engaging with them early during a crisis to explore opportunities for even just a retweet, or sharing of your crisis communications content, can go a long way toward reaching and influencing your specific audience. Ideally, you'll have established these networks before you need them. However, if you are a good corporate citizen with a truthful, authentic crisis response action plan, don't discount organisational crisis as an opportunity to engage with them.

Reflecting the changes in the way information is disseminated and consumed, a powerful blog or social commentary may now be your best way to reach those who need to hear your message most.

MY STORY: THE SYDNEY SIEGE: GOING ON THE NARRATIVE OFFENSIVE

> **Info Ops HQ** @InfoOpsHQ 🐦
> Appropriate the Police aren't sharing all available info. They are running a hostage rescue, not a news channel #SydneySiege #IOinAction
> 10:53 PM - 15 Dec 2014

When news broke on the morning of 15 December 2014 of a gunman holding hostages in a Sydney café, and news imagery soon showed some of those hostages being forced to hold up an Islamic flag against the café window, I naturally turned to Twitter to see what people were saying, reporting or theorising. I also tuned into the live stream of coverage from ABC News 24. I didn't switch off either channel until over 16 hours later, after the siege ended in the early hours of the following morning.

As is often the case in developing stories on which verified information is yet to be officially confirmed, a fair amount of conjecture was being reported by eyewitnesses, the news media and citizen journalists alike.

As is my inclination, I entered the online conversation to temper some of the misinformation being spread. As I've often lectured and blogged, speculation that sends social media hyperbole into overdrive does little to actually inform people. This critical incident was no different. Add into the equation elements of religious propaganda and tensions begin to simmer. Using Twitter as my primary channel, I adopted a 'verified' approach to reporting based on what I could view via the live feed or from sources that were basing their coverage on verified fact.

Most surprising as the siege went on was the restraint the Australian media showed in their adherence to the information embargo requests from the New South Wales Police Force. This was reflected not only in their refusal to broadcast or publish the demands and videos produced by the man at the centre of the crisis – Iranian-born Australian citizen and self-styled Islamic cleric Man Haron Monis – but also in their careful choice of words. Words that reflected those being communicated by the New South Wales Chief Police Commissioner and his deputy.

The word 'terrorism' was not adopted by the New South Wales Police Force or by the majority of Australian media. In fact, it wasn't until the global media in the UK, and later the US, covered the siege in their morning news cycles that the narrative shifted significantly.

From that point on not only were demands and videos broadcast, but Monis was given the 'terrorist' label he so desperately wanted. In his warped reality and with his newly forged allegiance with the

Islamic State of Iraq and the Levant, Monis was seeking a very public form of religious martyrdom. Just what neither the New South Wales Police Force nor the Australian media were willing to give him.

The posting on social media of the videos Monis had made with the hostages were of particular concern. The New South Wales Police Force had specifically requested that these videos not be published by the news media or shared by people on social media. Once the UK and US came online, though, his videos started littering the twittersphere.

I sent out numerous tweets on the hashtags in play explaining the Police's concerns. My response to people retweeting a video was to politely ask them to remove it. To be honest, I expected to cop an early-morning trolling for doing so. However, every single person I tweeted and asked to remove the offending video did so obligingly.

I was surprised by this. But I was more surprised by what happened next. Those same people started going through the hashtags in play, identifying and politely asking others to remove the video as well.

Before long there were a small but industrious bunch of Twitter users asking people to take down the videos they saw and reporting said videos to YouTube, who were exceptionally quick to remove them from their site.

As events came to a dramatic head shortly after 2 am, watching the police operation that unfolded live was exceedingly confronting.

The wait for verified information that followed the end of the siege saw a lull in speculation on Twitter. Bar a few news outlets speculating on the outcome, people simply didn't engage, instead praying for a positive outcome. Tragically, two hostages were killed and police shot Monis dead on site.

After covering the Sydney siege on Twitter in real time, I came away with two profound observations as a crisis communicator and military influence adviser:

1. *Small movements of people on Twitter can have a big impact.*

In this case, the dissemination of the videos Monis had made was prevented from gaining any social foothold on the hashtags in play.

Applying this beyond the siege to an organisational context, this suggests that small movements on Twitter can have significant influence of both a positive and negative nature.

The lesson? Don't ever discount the work of a small but industrious group of people on Twitter. They can be your biggest ally or biggest enemy, and their numbers may mean little.

2. *Local (or geographical) news embargos will not be respected by the international news media.* But does it matter?

While the Australian media largely kept to reporting fact and resisted the urge to sensationalise the incident, the narrative shift that occurred when the UK and US came online was profound. While on the surface you might think that would automatically send up a red flag in your organisational risk profile, the more I reflected on the shift in narrative the more I realised it was also a lesson in where your audience is not.

Realistically, how many Australians waited until 1 am when CNN and the UK's *Independent* started shifting the narrative? I would wager that very few Australians were using overseas news channels as their primary source of information on a siege that was nearing its 16th hour.

So, if all the action is happening in your geographic region, does it make any difference what people on the other side of the world are saying? Possibly yes, it does, if you are a global multinational; but also no, if you're a locally based organisation. In a crisis communications context, where you throw your communications resources matters.

While social media is predominantly a global entity, situational acuity, both geographically and in cyberspace, still plays a large role in who ends up *influenced by* your messaging.

In this case, Australians were influenced by Australian media sources and a very strong and exceptionally well executed crisis communications plan by the New South Wales Police Force, which included full exploitation of all their social media channels.

So, while keeping your eyes on the tweets of the world, don't get caught up in trying to influence people who don't matter to your audience in the crisis context in which you find yourself.

12

From battlefield to boardroom:
the art of social media influence

How persuasive a communicator do you think you are? Could you convince a CEO to break their own bad news? Tweet your way out of a crisis? Blog your way back from the organisational brink?

These skills are more important than you realise, because as the communications landscape has evolved, unless you're communicating with influence on networks where people are tuning in, you might as well be sending Morse code into outer space.

And yet the words *influence*, *persuasion* and *propaganda* have developed sinister connotations over time.

I understand why, but what I also see is the mainstream adoption of a *perception* toward these words that has been manufactured, largely by the news media and political fraternities, for the global information news cycle.

Think about it. Why is it that when you see these words associated with a person, a movement or a government you become sceptical of their motives?

By and large it's because these words have been deliberately used in association with individuals or regimes that provoke strong feelings of fear.

But being an effective influencer or persuader doesn't necessarily mean you're a raging, power-hungry fruit-loop with aspirations of world domination. There are myriad people who are effective influencers doing wonderfully positive and inspiring things.

If Steve Jobs wasn't an expert influencer, Apple Inc. would never have made it outside his father's garage. If Mark Zuckerberg wasn't an expert influencer, Facebook would never have left the halls of Harvard. If Melissa Mayer wasn't an expert influencer, Yahoo would be gathering dust on the same shelf as MySpace.

Similarly, not all propaganda is geared to mislead you. We sell the ideals of equal rights, tolerance, freedom and equality exactly the same way as, for example, terror and prejudice are communicated to us.

Influencers are by nature effective communicators.

Some people have a natural talent for influence and persuasiveness — we often refer to them as charismatic. But it's also a skill that can be learned.

Developing the perception of influence isn't without its challenges. Influence, particularly when widespread, is often attributed to gender, race, religion and many other characteristics that have little to do with the individual's ability to communicate and even less to do with their expertise.

As a personal example, having spent most of my working career in male-dominated environments, I've experienced numerous illogical references to my gender in the influence equation, even among female peers.

Assertiveness, and the ability to communicate concisely with influence, isn't socially palatable when combined with a bias perception. Take, for example, one of the biggest headline stories of 2014:

'George Clooney: Star marries Amal Alamuddin in Italy'

People Magazine

versus:

'Internationally acclaimed barrister Amal Alamuddin marries an actor'

Business Woman

Whether you identify as male, female or transgender, when your capability is tied to your gender, it's just an attempt to avoid overt gender bias. It's easy to label a woman as aggressive, for example, when she is simply being assertive in exerting influence in her area of expertise. It's not often you hear of a man being described in the same way. Why? Because that's the way perception works.

Crisis communicators need to remain acutely aware of the perception bias that audiences, the media and even internal stakeholders hold, both on an individual and an organisational crisis level.

Being able to identify these biases is critical to your ability to remediat and crises, to hose down the fire rather than fuel it.

Unless conspiracy theory or brand bashing is your aim, feeding people's perceptions and misconceptions is a gladiator's arena you want to stay well clear of. In the words of J.K. Rowling's Albus Dumbledore, 'Words are, in my not-so-humble opinion, our most inexhaustible source of magic. Capable of inflicting injury, and remedying it.'

Battlefield to boardroom: why social media needs to be part of your communications arsenal

A quick lesson from a military information operations adviser on symmetric warfare and its application to the boardroom:

> Symmetric warfare occurs when two adversaries share the same military powers and resources and rely on similar tactics. The only differentiating factor is how they deploy and execute those powers and resources to try to defeat their adversary.

> In the boardroom as on the battlefield, you are symmetrically matched to your adversaries on social media.

Whether you're present in the social media battlespace or marketplace is up to you. From a crisis communications perspective, a lack of presence on social media makes it much harder to manage organisational crises effectively.

You may produce all the right offline communications products, but someone else will be communicating them, or parts thereof, throughout social media, at which point you lose control of your own narrative. You're at the behest of citizen journalists and the news-selling media. You lose digital and social traffic. You lose the data sets that could help you monitor audience sentiment.

 Tweet this

In crisis comms a lack of presence on social media makes it much harder to manage organisational crises effectively #SMROE

By being absent from the social media conversation during crisis, you are fighting a symmetric war with an asymmetric mindset.

It's a war you cannot win.

For those in the boardroom, taking a leaf out of the military crisis and information operations doctrine is a socially savvy move. The process-driven nature of military organisations has consolidated the nuances of playing to win over decades, and you don't have to join the green machine to learn from their successes and failures.

Out of the rise of the Islamic State of Iraq and Levant was born a new form of conflict: social media jihad. The lesson here is simple: military organisations around the world were blindsided when these terrorists effectively weaponised social media.

The social networks that were built by Americans, with headquarters on American soil, are now being used as a weapon against Americans and their allies.

Instead of operating in a symmetric social battlespace, the west were still figuring out how to arm their tweets and deploy their blogs. In the interim, an information vacuum formed that fed the news media cycle with terrorist-generated content, which was precisely the terrorists' intent.

You need not start fighting a social media war or crisis from a position of strategic weakness. Take this lesson back to your boardroom: being present on social media in your marketplace well before any crisis arises gives you a strategic advantage when crisis does occur.

Don't leave the social media marketplace open to invasion from your competitors: be present, engage and build influence. Because when crisis hits, you will need to call on every ounce of goodwill you have built with your audience.

> 🐦 **Tweet this**
> Being on social media in your marketplace well before any crisis arises gives you a strategic advantage when crisis does occur #SMROE

BOARDROOM LESSONS IN CRISIS COMMUNICATIONS FROM THE BATTLEFIELD

- *Plan for war during peacetime.* Don't wait for a social media crisis to arise before putting in place a crisis communications plan.

- *Train for war during peacetime.* Big kudos for having a plan; now get into the mix and practise deploying it with your teams.

- *Never go to war without a strategy.* Know your organisational risks and plan your response ahead of time.

- *Leadership matters.* You're the boss, so *be* the boss. Be present, be available.

- *Expect flashback.* Someone somewhere will notice your social media crisis and try to ignite it with a blowtorch. Accept that it will happen. Don't focus on it. Your mission is crisis control.

- *Take advice.* Surround yourself with the experts you need and consider their advice carefully before making any decisions. Then give them the space to do what they've been trained to do.

- *Be voluntarily accountable.* It's your organisation—now is the time to own it. Don't wait for others to call you out on the elephant in the room.

Have a warrior ethos: don't leave anyone behind.

Your workforce and stakeholders should have your full attention during times of crisis. You are their leader and you need to do everything you can to bring them safely through an organisationally challenging time.

Only the victors write history ... oh and Wikipedia

#DidYouKnow many organisational crises have their own Wikipedia pages?

Fact. Think for a moment about who writes that history, because it's probably not your communications team.

Wikipedia, being an open source platform — *the free encyclopedia anyone can edit*', meaning truly *anyone, anywhere* — may be writing your organisational history. Are you okay with that?

I didn't think so.

While I don't recommend the Vladimir Putin approach to editing Wikipedia entries to suit your spin (the 'hire a small militia of PR people to spin things your way' approach), there are ways to ensure that what is written is more fact than fiction:

- Be truthful from the get-go. No cover-ups, no spinning the story sideways.

- Break your own news to control your own narrative.

- Monitor what is being said, not only on social media but also in the news media at large. If they aren't reporting fact, where has your messaging been lost? You may need to update your statements, tweet some corrections.

If you find that a Wikipedia page or entry is straying from the path of reasonableness, look carefully at where their listed sources of information are being pulled from.

For crisis communicators with a whopper on their hands, Wikipedia can tell you a lot about where your main media supporters and agitators are online. Small-time blogs and two-bit Tumblr commentary isn't generally cause for concern, but if those sources are coming up as major news outlets, or high-profile bloggers or are syndicated throughout news media outlets, this could indicate your crisis is not as contained as you thought it was. Or an active element of counter-crisis communications is going on.

Counter-crisis communications may take the form of targeted protest or activism, with groups of social media users or bloggers brand bashing your organisation deliberately. This often occurs during product boycotts and protest actions.

> 🐦 **Tweet this**
> Confrontation is not the answer; staying true to your course of
> deliberate, targeted, influential messaging is #SMROE

You may plan for an element of this. If it's pertinent to your risk profile, it's an extremely dynamic space that can quickly influence your audience sentiment if left unchecked. Confrontation is not the answer; staying true to your course of deliberate, targeted, influential messaging is.

Don't you know who I am? Why influence is the currency of the future

Influence in the 21st century has the unlikeliest of sources. Just a century ago, influence was the birthright of a few. For others it came about through the acquisition of money — lots of it. Today, entitlement by birth means little to most people, and anyone can make money. So what is the differentiating factor in the influence equation?

Welcome to the era of influence through building an online entourage.

From tweeps to fans to followers and subscribers, the size and quality of your online entourage gives others a general indication of your influence in a particular area of expertise.

By entourage quality, I refer to the influencers who generate large amounts of organic engagement, whose followers share their content without prompting.

An online influencer today usually has a savvy brand strategy that embraces all elements of social media (including video), podcasting, a strong web presence including a blog, perhaps a book or series of eBooks, and appearances at industry conferences and events. Their business is largely shaped by their entourage.

Most importantly from an organisational viewpoint, social media influence can build and engage an impassioned, cult-like following.

Take a look at just a few of the big influencers in their fields doing amazing things on social media:

- Virgin

- The Sea Shepherd Conservation Society

- GoPro

- The Israeli Defense Forces

- The United States Marine Corps

- Buddhist Boot Camp

- Firebrand Talent.

While some individuals behind these social powerhouses may be well known, their brands have appeal mainly because of their authentic and engaging manner. They're not 'brands' doing social media; they're brands telling their stories through their people with savvy social media strategists on their teams.

When crisis arises for these brands, and other organisations like them, they exert influence on a scale to ensure support rather than alienate their audience. If they have handled a social media crisis situation professionally, their audiences are likely to come to their defence before they've fired off their first statement. You can't buy that level of global influence — not through Google, not through the media.

It occurs organically and it takes time to build, but once established and maintained, corporate influence during times of crisis can be decisive in limiting damage to your organisation.

MY STORY: YES, MINISTER

As a former public servant, I worked through four federal elections and five prime ministers. I've been uninspired by each successive government and have often reflected on how I have been an unwilling scriptwriter in some of the political soap opera antics Australia has seen over the past decade or so.

In the lead-up to elections in particular, ministers love photo opportunities of the kissing babies, hand-shaking, tea-drinking type.

Better yet, let's get some soldiers in the photo, or a tank, or a plane, or a drug-sniffing dog. Or all four!

Above all, they like to announce 'new' things. And just as in the BBC series *Yes, Minister*, the hunt for *things* to announce becomes the stuff of public servant nightmares. I should know. I was kept awake at night by more than a few.

In the past three federal elections I found myself dreaming up things for ministers to announce. Like the time I was required to write a half-hour keynote speech that also had to 'announce something', even though the department had nothing newsworthy to announce. Let me tell you, dreaming up announceables on cue is not easy.

When there is no story to tell and no grounding in reality for the words you're meant to spin, authenticity flies out the window.

While the public may expect uninspiring speeches and publicity stunts from politicians, the same can't be said for the corporate sector. Even government departments and the military aren't immune from the necessity to make every announcement count – to mean something, offer value.

The lesson for crisis communicators here is simple: what you say primes your audience for what you say next. How you tell your stories primes your audience for what you do next.

If your organisation communicates for the sake of communicating, there is little value in the information cycle being created. It's like crying wolf: you churn out so much rubbish that when you actually have something meaningful to say, it's lost in the ether because people tuned out long ago.

Social influence means nothing if you've primed your audience over the long game with soft content. Because when you cry wolf (or vote for me!) everyone assumes it's just another selfie and scrolls on past.

The best stories are those that are based on truth and have a personal connection to the intended audience. Context is exceedingly powerful. Be engaging, be passionate, and above all be authentic.

PART II

THE PLAN IS TO HAVE A PLAN BEFORE YOU NEED A PLAN

Divine risk mitigation

Noah was a savvy guy. When God told him a flood was coming, he didn't sit about waiting for the rain to start. He built that ark and collected those animals. And Noah's forward strategy paid off.

Are you an ark builder? Or a good swimmer?

Why plan for risk?

Planning for risk is nothing new. We've been taught to plan for risk since infancy.

Learning to walk, run, ride a bike — all these formative risk situations taught us self-preservation in the simplest of ways. Fall over? Crash your bike? Someone is there to help you up and give you a cuddle.

By the time we are packed off to school, tangible consequences are part of the equation. Forget your lunch? Hungry is on the menu. Dog ate your homework? Huh?! Apparently they've heard that excuse before.

As we enter our teens, consequences have increasing meaning. Feelings and emotions embroil us in risk mitigation strategies. Regardless, we do stupid things like ride on motorbikes with boys (because he's cute rather than a safe driver) and drink cheap wine (because it's 'sophisticated' rather than enjoyable).

By the time we reach adulthood, perhaps with some further study behind us, and are in the workforce, we're paid to care and worry about other people's risks. The naivety of our youthful risk-taking behaviour and 'it won't happen to me' mentality is well behind us, and risk-and-consequence is something we do on autopilot.

So *why* is the idea of planning for social media risk so hard for people to grasp?

Examples of social media anarchy, social media meltdowns and corporate social media faux pas are plentiful. Yet even the sight of media sharks circling when there is blood in the water as the latest company flounders after a #PRFail isn't enough to convince decision makers to plan for social media risk.

My question is: Why *wouldn't* you plan for social media risk?

If your company sells its products online; if your government department uses social media as a customer service transactional platform; if your military unit uses it to generate publicity — you too could be starring in the latest #PRFail being broadcast in high definition around the world. Any time. Anywhere. Any post.

Planning for social media risk isn't any different from planning for any other business risks.

It's just the way those in leadership roles value (or devalue) social media that creates the perception of difference, and therein lies the biggest risk of all — organisational complacency.

> 🐦 **Tweet this**
> Planning for social media risk isn't any different from planning for any other business risks #SMROE

Creating a culture of social media risk awareness

'Why spend time and money planning for something that we have no control over?' I've heard many CEOs and government officials argue when talking about social media.

In my experience, the key to ensuring executive buy-in around social media (whether for crisis planning or business-as-usual adoption) is to talk to them in a currency that is meaningful to them. As a crisis communicator, whether civilian or military, you need to be able to identify your organisational leadership's currency (what matters most to them) and pitch your requests for support or planning overheads using terms of reference that will intrinsically resonate with them.

For corporations in the sales game, that looks like bottom-line equations of dollars and cents.

For the not-for-profit sector, that looks like volunteer manpower and donations (dollars and cents).

For military forces, the currency of the day is inextricably linked to your operational tempo and news media reporting cycle: this could mean reputational issues or it could mean public opinion and war support.

For government departments that are theoretically apolitical, the value proposition around the currency of communications is always linked back to the government of the day and their own communications strategy. While some political parties have a pro-engagement, all-in, the more publicity the better approach, others are risk adverse, sharing little or no information.

It is therefore unsurprising that government department communications tactics are driven by an alignment with the communication policies of the government, whose motivating communications currency is quite simply votes.

Think about what the communications currency is for your leadership group in this context and start cultivating organisational communications champions through meaningful internal communications engagement.

This is best achieved by asking leading questions that influence your executive into thinking about the issue in the terms of reference you have already established in your communications currency.

> 🐦 **Tweet this**
> Start cultivating organisational comms champions through meaningful internal comms engagement #SMROE

ARE YOU SPEAKING THEIR LANGUAGE?

Here are some of the ways I approach this:

- Outlining the dollars and cents equation of a consultant's billable hours and organisational manpower effort (time taken away from business as usual) in a planning versus reactive crisis management scenario, the former being exponentially cheaper than the latter.

(continued)

ARE YOU SPEAKING THEIR LANGUAGE? *(cont'd)*

- Emphasising the diversion of organisational resources during a crisis, which takes the public affairs or communications team away from business-as-usual activities such as sales and marketing. Dollars and cents aside, most organisations don't have an internal crisis communications expert on hand. They often find that their in-house communications team not only are ill-equipped to manage a social media crisis, but are overwhelmed with work on a resourcing front when crises do occur. That means that your internal resourcing cannot support their executives when they need it most.

- Highlighting that the cost of reputational damage is exceedingly hard to quantify, and that planning for risk mitigation and crisis communications ahead of time increases a leader's ability to effectively manage the incident (public perception) and remediate their reputation effectively. That means your leader is more likely to withstand the crisis than fall on their sword.

- And of course there is the envy factor: 'Would you take a look at what your competitors or adversaries are achieving on their social media channels!'

While you will find the C-Suite still exceedingly risk averse when it comes to social media, times are changing. As generations of digital natives start to break through the glass ceiling of corporate partnership and executive-level roles, they bring with them a new attitude toward social media.

This change is not without its challenges.

Digital natives and millennials are incredibly savvy to the ways of many consumers and stakeholders, but they don't know a world without social media and lack the overarching business acumen that generations of baby boomers and Gens X and Y have accumulated. In a transformational, innovative way, millennials bring an enormous amount to the boardroom;

but in a crisis communications situation, the lack of a holistic, whole-of-organisation view can lead to an over-reliance on social and online media as communications channels.

The trap is that each generation erroneously believes that the way to communicate to *everyone* is the way they have been generationally primed to be communicated to.

The truth is, you need to communicate to a range of generational stakeholders in a range of ways — and social media is not your one-stop communication shop.

Nor should it be.

Human factors

Never take the human factor out of planning for an organisational crisis response.

Whether it's in person in front of assembled media or in a video produced for YouTube, the talking head that becomes the face of your organisational crisis response is an essential element of crisis communications.

> 🐦 **Tweet this**
> Never take the human factor out of planning for an organisational crisis response #SMROE

There are circumstances where you may be able to get away with a Facebook apology while hosing down the Twitter stream of discontent, but when the proverbial really hits the fan, someone has to step up and face the public — in person.

What many leaders of both the baby boomer and younger generations fail to realise is that they are *the* most important person in the reputational risk equation.

Leadership, particularly in situations of crisis, is not an attribute forged when the fires are burning hot. It's an attribute developed over the long game. Building credibility and trust in your workforce, your shareholders and your government takes time. In a crisis, that's time you don't have.

To illustrate why you can't build leaders during a crisis, I've included some examples online at SMROE-HQ.

Conversely, I think it's important to share with you some examples of exceptional leadership, recognising individuals who remained unapologetically authentic during a crisis.

Richard Branson is perhaps one of the most polarising celebrity leaders of our time. His handling of two significant disasters in two very different areas of his business illustrates modern-day leadership at its authentic best. These were the Grayrigg Virgin train crash and the Virgin Galactic spacecraft crash.

In both cases, Branson was on the scene as quickly as possible, speaking with his people, speaking with the media and keeping the information flowing.

The lesson here is twofold:

1. Outcomes such as this can be achieved only through detailed, organisational crisis communications planning. Leaders must believe passionately in what they are doing and saying to make this work.

2. Branson's innate humanity is what enables him to connect with his audiences and the general public time and time again. This is something he is exceptionally good at. Do not attempt to change the leadership style of a person during a crisis. If your chosen talking head doesn't have the ability to communicate outside the confines of regulatory jargon, legalese or fluent bureaucracy, they aren't the right person for the job.

> 🐦 **Tweet this**
> Do not attempt to change the leadership style of a person during a crisis #SMROE

The runaway general

The well-publicised interview with General Stanley A. McChrystal (retired) in the July 2010 issue of *Rolling Stone* that led to his resignation offers a unique narrative of leadership during a career embedded in crisis management — only for that career to come to a stunningly abrupt end due to a crisis.

The lesson here: if you are in public office — whether civilian or military — don't tick off your political masters. No matter how great a leader you are or how terrific a job you are doing, you're on borrowed time when you speak out against the government of the day. Yes, even in 'democracies'. Public servants and the military are meant to be apolitical — but of course that really means being amenable to the government of the day (to the point you won't upset them), regardless of your own views.

'If that does not suit you, then get out!'

I doubt Lieutenant General Morrison ever contemplated becoming a YouTube sensation during his impressive career trajectory. But with over 1.5 million views of his 12 June 2013 video on investigations into allegations of sexual misconduct by Australian Army members, he won not only the undivided attention of the Australian Defence Force, but also news headlines around the world.

The lesson here is in his authenticity and passion. Did you observe the anger in General Morrison's face? The terseness in his voice? The veins straining on his forehead? That's the look of a leader who is serious about what he is saying. He believes it to his core, and this kind of personal conviction translates well on camera. Displays of emotion (when appropriate to the context of the crisis) humanise the speaker in a way that reaches people. Social media is primed for this kind of communications delivery.

A cautionary note: if you're thinking, 'Fabulous, we'll add a cookie cutter–style YouTube video as a crisis communications tool', think again.

It is very difficult to fake personal integrity and conviction, along with all the appropriate body language cues, convincingly. Many have tried. I can't think of one who has succeeded.

Leaving behind a library of cringeworthy examples in her wake, the former Republican Party Vice-Presidential nominee Sarah Palin has stumbled her way through dozens of media interviews. I've included some examples at SMROE-HQ. They make for exceedingly uncomfortable viewing. While many might blame her advisers for failing to prepare her for each interview, if she had been personally passionate about the political issues she was discussing or the reasons why a change of government was needed, she would have been able to communicate them convincingly and even sell them, regardless of her ignorance of the subject matter.

I hope staged videos with talking heads pretending to care about your crisis are now off your crisis communications strategy list!

Before I finish this section on why organisations should plan for risk, I'd like you to look back at all the examples given. Notice that most relate to home-grown crises? I didn't deliberately stack the deck in my favour here; it is a true reflection of the source of most organisational crisis.

> 🐦 **Tweet this**
> Take staged videos with talking heads pretending to care about your crisis off your crisis communications strategy list! #SMROE

Statistics commonly suggest that around 80 per cent of crises arise out of internal issues such as management negligence, incompetence or product/service failures. This list is by no means exhaustive, but as a general rule, more often than not crises emerge from issues not dealt with appropriately or risks not anticipated and planned for from within the walls of your own organisation. That leaves an estimated 20 per cent of crises arising from factors outside your organisation's control.

I don't know about you, but as a CEO I don't particularly like those odds.

I'd rather plan for the 80 per cent of things I can anticipate ahead of time, rather than see how long my communications team can tread water.

What to plan for

If I had a dollar for every time I was asked by an organisation *what* they should be planning for in terms of social media organisational or military information risk, I would be permanently sitting on a beach in Maui sipping ice-cold drinks with cute little umbrellas in them.

I'm no aeronautical engineer, and anyone with any measure of common sense would never let me fly a real plane (I can't even get a plane airborne in a simulator!), but I know that the risks associated with aviation-based organisations start with ticked-off passengers with flight delays and end with catastrophic disaster.

Similarly; I know zip about the finance sector but enough to understand that if the ATM, point-of-sale or internet banking system goes loco and people can't access or spend their money, the bean counters panic as customers run bank branches out of cash.

In a war zone? I don't need to tell you that crisis starts with gun battles and ends in a nation's tears.

You already know what risks your organisation faces. You really do. You are best placed to know all the touchpoints of your business where interactions could lead to risk.

The best way to approach mapping out these risks is by using a matrix-style register. Your assessment and scaling of risk comparative to your organisational transactions should follow the paradigm of rating the risk to:

1   threats to life

2   threats to property

3   threats to the environment.

You, along with your colleagues (the experts in your work areas, not the communications team!), need also to rate the risks according to a matrix such as the example in table A.

Table A: Rating organisational risks

Likelihood	Consequences				
	INSIGNIFICANT	MINOR	MODERATE	MAJOR	CATASTROPHIC
EXTREME	High	High	Extreme	Extreme	Extreme
HIGH	Medium	High	High	Extreme	Extreme
MEDIUM	Low	Medium	Medium	High	Extreme
LOW	Low	Low	Medium	High	Extreme
RARE	Low	Low	Medium	High	High

As your social media crisis communications strategy needs to encompass *all* the risks your organisation can face, and what the communications tools and strategies for each risk will look like, it's important to establish a risk register.

When compiling your list think about:

• natural disasters

• environmental disaster (via direct or indirect association)

• epidemics

• terrorism

• civil unrest indirectly affecting you (such as protests or riots)

• civil unrest directly affecting you (such as boycotts, workplace invasions or blockades)

- technology failure (yours)
- technology failure (your suppliers')
- mechanical failure (anything you own, use or operate, or with which your brand is associated)
- customer service failures
- leadership failures
- rumour and innuendo
- media misreporting.

Think geographically

Your organisational headquarters may be in Virginia Beach, but your offices and customers could be all around the world. What do your products and their geographical location have in common for every risk you have listed? What differences are apparent? Local staff will be able to extrapolate most of this information for you, as they know their own communities best.

Think about infrastructure

How will you communicate in the event of a power blackout or internet outage? How might you reach and re-establish communications for your offices in different geographical areas with varying degrees of infrastructure reliability?

How will you communicate if your social media streams are hacked? Do you have alternate operational accounts available?

How quickly can you turn off any social media posts you have scheduled in tools such as Hootsuite and Buffer[1] to transition to crisis communications?

Think about guilt by brand association

If you build, sell and/or lease products, you may experience crisis communications collateral damage if one of your customers has a mishap or disaster involving your product.

---

1. http://nicolematejic.com/my-village-of-support/my-social-toolbox

In the aviation sector, for example, aircraft manufacturers know that while they are not at the controls of an aircraft during an emergency or disaster, or immune to the weather or other 'acts of God', in the event of an incident questions will always be asked about the aircraft's build, maintenance and history.

As another example, high-end brands employ celebrities as brand ambassadors, making clear associations between brand and public personality; when that public figure is embroiled in a scandal it is the brand that suffers the most. While a celebrity's huge social media following is great from a marketing point of view, it's a quagmire in a crisis.

What guilt by association risks may your organisation run? It may be prudent to keep a risk register and profile — with or without pre-prepared contingency strategy — for each client.

Social media can make these crises inordinately more newsworthy than they otherwise might be — leading to a brand's overexposure or, worse, consumer backlash.

Don't forget the Zombie Apocalypse!

The White House has a Zombie Apocalypse plan. Yes, really!

While it's used as a training scenario to avoid a 'real-life' scenario causing undue panic, its existence sends a clear message that the White House plans for every conceivable permutation of risk.

You should too.

I'm not saying go out and pitch a Zombie Apocalypse plan to your boss! What I'm saying is if you think there is even the remotest possibility that a risk could eventuate, then it should be on your risk register as something to consider planning for.

Risk registers

You can find one of my risk register templates at SMROE-HQ.[2]

When completing the template of all your organisational risks and corresponding communications strategies, it's important always to think

---

2. http://www.socialmediarulesofengagement.com/smroe-hq/downloads

beyond the communicator's paradigm. That is, you need to wear your whole-of-organisation hat to identify your risks, and wear your crisis communicator's hat only when applying risk mitigation strategies and tactics.

Make a routine habit of cultivating resources in areas of the business you don't understand from both technical or business viewpoints. Draw on the knowledge of experts in the workplace: they know better than anyone what their risks are and how you can help them manage any communications crisis that arises.

The crisis communicator's go-bag[3]

If you had to leave your office in under 10 seconds, what would you take with you? Would you reach for your handbag or iPhone? Grab your wallet and keys?

Early on in my days running surveillance I picked up a trick from a Special Forces soldier turned spook, who introduced me to the concept of a 'go-bag'. It's a concept that applies to *any* vocation, *any* place, *any* where. As a crisis communicator, here's what's in mine:

- MacBook (always fully charged)

- MacBook powerpack

- iPad mini

- iPhone (which doubles as a mobile wi-fi network)

- iPhone/iPad charger cables and power packs

- battery extender packs (fully charged, for both iPad and iPhone)

- access to all social network and online account passwords and logins. I have these encrypted electronically on some of my devices. If I need to carry a hard copy I use old-school cryptography methods to protect the information.

- at least two muesli bars

- wallet, keys, sunglasses

- meds/painkillers

---

3. http://nicolematejic.com/my-village-of-support/my-crisis-comms-gobag

- pens, paper, business cards

- basic toiletries.

If I'm working interstate or overseas, other things you'll find in my (larger) go-bag are:

- GoPro (spare battery and charger)

- change of clothes, hat

- bottled water

- passport and stash of cash

- comprehensive first-aid kit.

Having a go-bag ready for your communications team should they have to bug out (military slang for get out quickly) is essential if your crisis communications plan requires them to remain in touch on the go while outside the office but inside a crisis. Many organisations use a type of go-bag for operators who work after hours or over weekends.

In one of my roles within Customs and Border Protection, during development of the business continuity plan for my work area the unit go-bag evolved into a hardened, lockable go-case with wheels. This provided not only for the volume of equipment that unit operators needed when they bugged out, but also the space to dump and lock up any working documents they had to take with them.

Think laterally about what might work for your workplace, including any information or operational security policies that need to be considered, and make sure your go-bag or go-case is light enough for anyone to carry or roll.

Building your ark

Build shit. Don't bullshit.

Scott Kilmartin

Ark construction should be approached like an assembly project rather than using a 'building it from the ground up' approach. Social media isn't a linear process. You need to build your ark to be dynamically responsive to the changing nature of online media and put tools in place to monitor audience sentiment actively, in real time.

That dirty S word: strategy

A strategy is to a plan what Noah was to his Ark. Noah had a plan; but before he had a plan he had a strategy.

God told Noah a great flood was coming and he should build an ark and collect breeding pairs of animals. So Noah started to think about how he could accomplish this task. How would he build an ark that could accommodate all those different animals and withstand a flood?

If he didn't allow for all the different type of animals, the ark might have sunk under the weight of the elephants, or the giraffes would have had a hard time finding headroom.

The *thinking* part, or strategising, was a critical factor in Noah's ability to turn an idea into action and then a positive outcome. Once he had set his strategy, he then went about the 'doing' or tactical part — the *actual building* of the ark.

Having an overarching social media strategy that guides your plan — or the doing part of crisis communications work — is essential in managing crisis communications. Much as Noah planned to ensure the Ark didn't sink and the giraffes could fit inside, you need to do the *thinking* work of managing a crisis before the *doing* part of your response.

This is particularly critical when social media is part of your crisis, whether as cause or solution.

Your communications strategy will most likely form part of your organisation's overall business strategy. That is, it is a part of an all-encompassing organisational document that was developed to ensure all facets of the business work together in harmony and toward the same goals.

This is an important starting point for crisis communicators because it is essential that the crisis communications strategy, and the plans it sets out, be in harmony with what is happening in the rest of the organisation. See figure A for an illustration.

Figure A: embarrassment for the Israeli Defence Force

Gregg Carlstrom @glcarlstrom
Israeli army calls up thousands of reservists to simulate war w/Hezbollah; forgets to tell defense minister, Knesset bit.ly/18caTmm
7:50 PM - 01 Mar 2013

While there is no doubt the Israeli Defence Force is among the world's finest, the sort of strategic oversight that resulted in this rather significant, organisationally embarrassing error is a fairly common one.

As is often the case, the sexy of the situation is what people focus on most. Whether that's the rolling out of a new car from the production line or sending soldiers to war, it's sad but true that touchpoints such as communications are given less priority and organisational attention than they are due. Informing a minister of, well, almost anything is not a particularly popular task.

In this case, however, the job of informing the government about the war games going on that everyone forgot to tell them about would be especially unenviable!

Sadly this isn't an isolated case. I've seen situations like this occur repeatedly within government departments, particularly in sections of the organisation that have 'grown their own' communications teams outside the normal strategic communications and public affairs structures.

Strategic oversight

In theory, for leaders to develop their own communications assets is a savvy strategic move, but it can also create conflicting hierarchies. This is particularly evident in organisations with a split military–civilian or law enforcement–civilian workforce.

To whom exactly do leaders report? Those in uniform may have a Chief of Service to report to, who in turn may have an administrative civilian master. Their administrative reporting lines may be clear, but uniform loyalties make this a scenario where many feel as if they are being pulled in two separate directions.

How do you keep everyone happy?

While private sector organisations won't (necessarily) be sending reservists into the streets on war simulations, similar issues can arise in different contexts. The most common disconnect I see is between teams of people who perform similar functions within the organisation, such as customer service staff and social media managers.

Instead of having a holistic strategy across teams who have like functions in the workplace, there still exists a corporate predilection for the devolution of like skills into single sets of discrete job families.

The customer service team is geared toward complaint management, but they don't necessarily have a real-time view of those same customers using social media to publically air grievances already raised. The social media managers take on an aspect of complaint management, only to find that the customer service team are already dealing (or have dealt) with the same individual. It's like a toddler playing one parent off against the other to achieve a better outcome for themselves.

It's not social media that makes scenarios such as these possible — it's a lack of strategic oversight. This makes having a social media strategy critical to mission success.

Forget about the tactical *how* for the time being and focus on strategic *connectivity*. As a crisis communicator, you need to be able to identify these points of weakness and influence organisational change to remedy the situation.

It could be as simple as suggesting a change management activity to optimise and rationalise resourcing; or it could be more complex and involve staff retraining and redeployment.

Regardless of how you connect each sector of the organisation or business to the others in your social media crisis communications strategy, you must have fundamental lines of communication embedded in your checklists for effective stakeholder liaison.

I'm a huge advocate of crisis communications strategy checklisting — one, because it's methodical and forces you to go through your strategy project management style line by line; and two, because it translates directly into the output of planning.

Like a pilot's pre-flight checklist, it's your 'good-to-go' inventory for before you fly into a social media nightmare. This approach enables you to both cultivate strategic foresight and be dynamically and tactically responsive to the demands of a social media crisis.

It bridges the divide between the strategy, for example of planning for simulated warfare, and the tactical action captured in a checklist line that reads, say:

Serial 1. 30 days before simulation: Advise Defence Minister of intent to …

Tips and tricks

I've found the app Evernote[4] particularly useful for crisis communications (and general) strategic planning, particularly for organisational teams running across multiple locations and time zones.

Evernote enables you to create notebooks in different categories and to stack (file) notes. The beauty of Evernote here is that you can quickly navigate to the strategy you require, drill down into the tactical planning aspects of how to manage organisational crisis, and send those instructions or that checklist immediately to the person who needs it. It's like a visual rolodex in place of pages of PDFs or old-school reams of paper in folders. Notes or checklists can be emailed, PDF-ed or worked on from a smartphone, tablet or desktop device, making this an exceptionally diverse mobile solution.

It is also an incredible social media and web savvy tool. You can capture web pages, pictures, posts or tweets and add them into notes for collaborative discussion and decision making.

Evernote has API connectivity with accounting and time management software such as Xero, so you can also quickly ascertain how much time you are spending on each task, or what your billable hours are looking like.

Building your crew

A qualified and highly motivated crew is essential for any ship sailing toward storms.

Ahoy Captain!

Every ark needs a captain. Who will your Noah be? Who will be your public face during your crisis? Title or rank doesn't translate into social media crisis communications success. 'CEO' doesn't impress twenty-somethings, and having a two-star general deliver messaging to troopers can guarantee disengagement.

Your talking head should be able to connect authentically with your organisational audience in quick time. This could be because they already have a social media presence or public profile your audience is familiar with;

---

4. http://nicolematejic.com/my-village-of-support/my-social-toolbox

or it could be because their position defines how people will receive or 'consume' the information they have to share.

If you think of this in military terms, there is a reason why sergeants-at-arms communicate with the troops below them in rank while officers are largely kept out of the mix. They know their audience, and they have an authentic and credible way of communicating through pre-existing channels. Adopt a similar sensibility in determining who is best suited to the role of captain of your ark.

Your captain is responsible for one thing during a crisis: publicly navigating through the inevitable sea of discontent.

As a crisis communicator, you may well also be the organisational face of a crisis, but more often you are the driving force behind the captain's actions and words. It's important that the delineation of roles and responsibilities here is clear.

An organisation's CEO may not be the right person for the job. Not only must your captain be able to lead the organisation through crisis, but they must also be able to withstand media questioning and public scrutiny. It's not a role everyone is comfortable with.

The XO

On a naval ship the Executive Officer (or XO) is the captain's trusted adviser and deputy. The XO provides the captain with frank and fearless advice, challenging their logic and preparing them for any public interactions.

The XO also ensures the crew are prepared for crisis and ready to perform to the required standards during a crisis. Above all, the XO has the captain's back, meaning they have their captain's best interests at heart.

The XO is responsible for:

- ensuring the crew (team) are prepared for a crisis
- ensuring the crew execute instructions provided during a crisis in a timely manner
- proofreading tweets, posts and other communiqués before they are cleared for release
- acting as a sounding board for ideas within the team and for the captain
- liaising with internal stakeholders to obtain information

- liaising with the crisis communications team on behalf of the captain to ensure the plan is being followed and implemented

- acting responsively to changes in social media audience sentiment, including escalating matters to the captain.

Above all, the XO is a problem solver who routinely offers solutions.

Beam me up, Scotty!

Everyone's favourite ship's engineer (okay, *Star Trek*'s USS *Enterprise* is technically a spaceship, but bear with me for the purposes of the analogy!), Montgomery Scott had a proactive attitude toward solving problems on the fly. You need an engineering department with the same problem-solving ethos onboard your ark to do the following:

- Manage IT infrastructure — You can expect organisational web traffic to increase significantly during a crisis as people hunt for information, so make it easy for them to find it. This may require being able to update websites and put in place redirects in quick time. It must include responsive web solutions for mobile and tablet viewing.

- Monitor and manage any attempts at cyber intrusion on your organisational network.

- Ensure your devices are mobile ready and you have multiple internet connectivity options (if required).

Coxswains and deckhands

Your social media coxswains and deckhands are your most versatile team members. They are often drawn from areas such as communications, marketing and public affairs, but you may find resources in other areas helpful in times of niche crisis. For example, if the crisis concerns human resources or industrial relations, having a knowledgeable deckhand on your team with that expertise will be extremely helpful. Social media deckhands are responsible for:

- monitoring social media audience sentiment and alerting the XO (or captain) to risk

- making sure all organisational record-keeping obligations are being met (this can be particularly important and daunting in some organisations, but may also be a legal requirement)

- curating the social media conversation
- driving social engagement and shareability (if appropriate)
- responding to inbound media enquiries (and having responses ready for clearance)
- providing administrative assistance
- managing the organisation's day-to-day business affairs
- providing niche content expertise (if required).

While many organisations are structured hierarchically, they rarely work this way in a practical sense. Commonly there is a natural cross-pollination of business functions and outcomes shared between departments or work areas in a very lateral way.

Establishing clear roles and responsiblities in each organisational work area and for each ark crew member during a crisis ensures everyone is singing the same tune when and where it matters most.

Planning for the flood

Anyone can hold the helm when the sea is calm.

Publilius Syrus

The rain has started and you can hear the thunder rolling in. How do you keep dry and stay afloat on social media during the crisis communications flood?

One word: planning.

With your strategy closely aligned to your organisational objectives, and your risk matrix completed, you can now get into the tactical *how* of managing your social media crisis.

From deploying a social media command centre to running through your checklists, here are the top issues you will need to plan to address during common social media crises.

The apology

Sorry. It's one of the most powerful and authentic words you can use. Say it publicly (if appropriate), say it early, say it often.

And mean it. Don't hide it in paragraphs of nonsensical blah blah blah. Don't try to spin the story another way while sneaking it in at the end. Own the narrative of your apology; don't make people go looking for it.

In my experience, this is one of the hardest outcomes to achieve for a crisis communicator, but it's something I truly believe is the right course of action. Why? Because authenticity is key. If you can't deliver an authentic apology, how convincingly can you really spin a lie?

> **🐦 Tweet this**
> Own the narrative of your apology; don't make people go looking for it #SMROE

Social media audiences have an endless variety of information sources at their disposal, and if they smell a rat they will call your bluff. Most lies lack objective evidence to support them. What then?

Don't place your organisation in a position of no-reply. By that I mean if you don't apologise and settle a matter appropriately, you are effectively handing the keys to the karma bus to those you have wronged.

If you don't control the narrative of your apology on *your* terms, when the truth comes out, as it inevitably will, not only will you have little to no warning of imminent social warfare, but you will by default be placed in a defensive, retaliatory position. And laws around privacy and professional codes of conduct may even prevent you from responding in the way you would like.

Not to mention you'll look extra sinister for mishandling the issue in the first place, or for trying to cover it up.

The mistake

Fess up. Admit it. You screwed up. You could have handled that situation better. Take responsibility for your part in how things have developed to the point where you have to activate your social media crisis communications plan.

Keeping your audience's respect during a crisis should be your primary concern. Don't risk making an already bad situation worse. If you spin your story in a dishonest way, the truth will inevitably come out eventually and then you will be in for crisis round two *and* look extra deceitful. Your audience trust levels will go into free-fall, making it exceedingly hard for you to recover.

You can admit your mistake without admitting fault (this is the part to show your lawyer).

Empathising with the way people feel, regardless of who is at fault, shows you care about your stakeholders and you have heard what they've said. This isn't an admission of guilt or posturing toward taking blame. It's a simple act of humanity that has an enormously powerful potential to de-escalate high-stakes, tense and emotional situations.

Making sure reaching out in a human way is part of your social media response to crisis is essential in maintaining an authentic, sincere narrative.

Showing organisational compassion, offering a sincere apology for a situation gone awry, shows far more moral fortitude and corporate conviction than staying silent or, worse, hiding behind a veil of bureaucracy and taking a hostile defensive position.

Use your words objectively and with intent.

> 'We appreciate your taking the time to tell us about the way X situation made you feel …'

> 'We are sorry to hear that X situation made you feel disappointed/hurt/angry … That was never our intent.'

Avoid using words that frame your position defensively and fail to acknowledge the feelings of the person or group you are responding to. Avoid emotionally subjective descriptors and keep your response professionally aligned with the core values and beliefs of your organisation.

More often than not, complainants on social media simply want to be heard and acknowledged. It is very difficult for people to stay angry with others, or with an organisation, when the responses they receive are delivered with mindful kindness.

The lessons learned

Be quick to learn from your crises. The concept of *time* is irrelevant in social media. What might spark a crisis in a moment might also smoulder for some time before igniting (or reigniting).

Are you about to make the same mistake again? How did this crisis occur?

How are you preventing it from occurring again? Don't be blind to the contributions made by your own people to the situation you find your organisation in.

Many crisis communicators who work on retainer or contract are one step removed from internal organisational politics. Managers who cannot remove their corporate blinkers are a massive hindrance to resolving crises.

Crisis communicators who face off against managers and leadership teams who refuse to be accountable for the role their staff plays in creating crises are quite simply going to find themselves in a never-ending cycle of social media whiplash.

You might think this is great for repeat business, but a word of warning. Once is unlucky, twice is forgiven, but by the third time you're being called in to fix the same social media disaster they still won't be reflecting on their actions and/or inactions — they'll be pointing the finger of failure in your direction.

A critical skill I learned early in my career as a Customs and Border Protection officer is that it is impossible to negotiate with irrational people. Similarly, it is impossible to reason with people who are unwittingly incompetent, who have been promoted beyond their leadership skills and who simply don't have the ability actually to *manage* their teams. In these cases, lessons will never be learned.

Keep the clients who have the strategic vision to accept your impartial professional view; break up with those who call you a third time for the same problems. That may sound harsh, but as a crisis communicator your reputation and credibility depend on your delivering successful outcomes. You cannot achieve this if your professional advice is being thrown to the wind in ignorance or arrogance.

There is a world of difference between leaders who take your advice into consideration and those who blatantly ignore it. In these situations, the lesson learned during a crisis could very well be yours.

Measures of scale

Knowing your social media audience's sentiment around a crisis is critical to being able to scale your response accordingly.

Ideally you need to match your crisis response to the scale of their outrage. Too heavy and it may appear as if you are overcompensating, which translates into suspicion (are you 'protesting too much'), too little and your response may be viewed as uncaring and inadequate.

Knowing when to communicate, when to stay silent and when to engage is a delicate balancing act. You can use social media behavioural indicators to help here.

> 🐦 **Tweet this**
> Knowing when to communicate, when to stay silent and when to engage is a delicate balancing act #SMROE

SOCIAL MEDIA BEHAVIOURAL INDICATORS

Online community self-moderation

Are your fans or tweeps already curating the discussion and standing up for your organisation or product? It's time to communicate and engage.

The lone wolf

If your crisis revolves around a single person with a single grievance, a direct approach may work best. Take the conversation offline and engage with kindness (while keeping a record of any conversation).

The gang

One person may start a personal war (with or without a legitimate grievance) and then invite their friends to join in to 'boycott' or brand bash your organisation. This can start off with a few people but can grow exponentially. You must quickly assess whether the complainant's goal is to lure you into a social media stoush. This is not the time for engagement. It's the time for a single statement and then silence. Say your piece, then say nothing.

The troll

The trolls I remember as a child of the eighties were cute with brightly coloured fuzzy hair. Sadly, online trolls are more like their gruesome namesakes in *The Hobbit*. Trolls are interested only in causing mischief to provoke you. They're like the schoolyard bully who is simply looking for a fight and picks the easiest target. There is absolutely no point in engaging with them. Report and block them wherever possible. If you give them enough oxygen, they can cause real distress to your communications and social media teams too.

These definitions and recommended responses should be used as a guide, but the dynamic nature of social media and crisis communications will require you to remain responsive to the scale and sentiment of your audience in different situations. Don't be afraid to keep your crisis management style fluid to remain responsive, shifting between strategies as the crisis evolves.

Attention to detail

Have your grammar and spelling checked, and scan photographs and videos for embarrassing visual blunders. At a time of heightened audience vigilance and criticism, don't give people more ammunition by making silly mistakes. Check that people's names are spelt correctly and the right gender inflections are used. If you aren't sure, find out.

When responding to social media–based complaints make sure you actually address the specific complaint in your response. Sounds obvious but this is often overlooked. Providing the complainant with a brilliant account of your policy but no answer to their particular grievance only creates more social media ire.

Running a competition? If the conditions are specific, such as 'entries must be 25 words or less', make sure the winning entry complies before announcing and publishing the results.

Before a written apology goes to print, ask to see a copy of the page layout, keeping in mind the synergy of surrounding headlines and ads to avoid any further gaffes. Print placement should be at the top of your agenda if you want to head off the risk of collateral damage at the hands of an editor who is in the business of selling news, even if turns into your next crisis.

Are your crisis communications aligned? Does your 140-character message on Twitter accord with your messaging on Facebook, Google+ and LinkedIn? Crisis communications should be consistent. If there isn't enough room in a tweet to say what you need to say, work those URL links! Use your social channels to drive traffic to where you want your crisis engagement or calls-to-action to occur. This could be the whole web or a single social media network.

Don't auto-post from one network to another. Take the time to carefully craft a message for each one.

> 🐦 **Tweet this**
> Use your social channels to drive traffic to where you want your crisis engagement or calls-to-action to occur #SMROE

Legal eagles

Seek early legal advice on issues that could cause you grief. This includes breaches of industry codes of conduct or practice. The first call your executive receives to advise them of any potential legal ramifications should be from their own advisers, not the governing body or the media.

Avoid at all costs deferring to the language used by lawyers in issuing apologies or statements. Social media audiences are allergic to bullshit, and no one wants to read legalese in 140-character bursts; the only thing you'll achieve is alienating your audience further.

If your organisation has an in-house legal team, involving them in your planning and war gaming is time exceptionally well spent. Not only does this build good corporate citizenship, but it also gives both you as a communicator and them as experts in the law the opportunity to learn to work with one another to achieve mutually agreeable outcomes.

> 🐦 **Tweet this**
> Social media audiences are allergic to bullshit, and no one wants to read legalese in 140-character bursts #SMROE

You might also find that they bring a valuable set of risk indicators to the planning cycle, as they often have a unique overview of the whole organisational transactional business.

Tapping specialist internal resources such as the legal team can be valuable in identifying or scaling risks that might otherwise go unnoticed.

Be social

Arguably the worst decision to make when dealing with a social media crisis is to withdraw and go socially silent, like an ostrich burying its head in the sand. By doing so you're missing a prime opportunity for genuine engagement with your audience.

I can guarantee you that remaining social will be a hard sell to your organisational leadership group. Their instinctive reaction will be to hide and hope that the media don't sniff around too much, to spin the truth sideways or to play defence before the game has even started.

These scenarios should worry you. Ordinarily, karma is a bitch. Social media karma is an epic bitch.

Don't hand the keys to the karma bus to those most affected by your crisis. They will run you down one social network at a time and then refuel that bus, pick up more social media passengers and keep on driving until *they* are ready to stop. Then they'll park the bus for a while and bring it out every now and then to remind you of that one time you had a crisis.

So instead of pretending your crisis doesn't exist or spinning it like the DJ at a rave party, embrace it — tackle it head on and *own* the narrative.

Better yet, break the bad news yourself and take control of the narrative in a proactive, authentic way. Show your audience you care enough to talk to them about your crisis — preferably before the media breaks the story. Engage the social trust and goodwill you have already accumulated and demonstrate your resolve to remedy the situation with leadership and accountability.

As Henry Kissinger famously said, 'If it's going to come out eventually, better have it come out immediately' — on your terms.

Drills and skills

When a navy commissions a new ship, lots of sea trials and testing take place. Once the ship is deemed seaworthy, the crew arrives and then they drill some more. It's not because they don't have faith in their new ship; it's because all skills, no matter how easy or complex, require practice.

Everyone who joins an organisation goes through a boot camp of sorts. You might not have had the shoe-polishing, marching and push-upping kind of workplace induction that those in the military are familiar with, but you will have been acclimatised to your workplace in some way. From introductions, office tours and orientation sessions to online training and offline courses, you would have been required to practise your skills with some supervision before being let loose in your new job.

Ark boot camp is just the same.

Getting together the core team who will manage a crisis to practise implementing the social media crisis communications plan, going through some scenarios and lessons learned, and reviewing what has been happening in the #PRFail world at large, is critical to organisational success during a crisis.

You don't have to live through your own #PRFail. Learning from the mistakes of others, in a social media context, is an exceptionally savvy approach to ensuring potential risks are identified and your organisational teams are prepared.

Navigation

Navigating through a crisis is much like a Choose Your Own Adventure book. Decision makers are essentially plotting the narrative for the forthcoming chapters in your organisational adventure, hopefully toward a return to business as usual.

But navigation is a skill that is learned; and crisis communicators, by virtue of being the advisory point in an organisational crisis, need to master the art of navigation through rough seas.

The first rule of navigation is to have a map. What is your plan? Where do you want to go? How are going to get there? And how are you going to move your audience with you from point A to point B?

The second rule of navigation is to know where you are. Where within your crisis communications plan are you starting this journey? You might be in the pre-crisis management phase or you might have the media camped out on your front lawn.

The third rule of navigation is to keep an eye on the weather. You know where you're starting from and you've got your plan, but sometimes storms will blow in and make sailing your planned course unfeasible. It's time to reassess your plan and chart a new sailing route.

So you know where you are, you have a map and you've got the weather channel streaming on your iPhone. What else do you need to look out for?

Using social media as a crisis communications tool to navigate your way through or away from disaster has its quirks, not least of which is the humans at the helm while the ship takes a battering.

Human bias and the cult of social media celebrity create a hive-like mentality of hysteria that feeds on likes, retweets and shares.

A swift and decisive change in social media community moderation and content creation is required during a crisis. You need to ensure the organisation isn't still stuck in a business-as-usual mindset. Without this change in mindset within your workforce, you run the very real risk of organisational shipwreck.

Here are some lessons to be learned from social media shipwrecks.

1. Iceberg! Dead ahead

You may think you have the most infallible product and crisis communications strategy around, but make sure you have someone keeping watch for risks on the horizon.

Don't underestimate the size of the crisis. It may look like a small ice mass, but the real danger could lie underwater; or in an organisational sense, the weakest corporate link will often be the first to show signs of failure. This could be anything from poor leadership to disgruntled employees to unhappy customers to share market ripples.

2. Sail-pasts are never a good idea

Crisis management should not be about anything other than managing the crisis. A peculiar aspect of using social media in managing crises is the innate desire to gather symbols of social validation (likes, retweets and so on) as a way of demonstrating messaging cut-through and saturation.

While social media can be used effectively in a crisis, there needs to be a distinct shift away from the posting-for-likes mindset that is prevalent during business-as-usual operations. The shareability of your content must be inherent, not an overt cue. Crisis content must provide information of value to your audience.

Showing off with witty banter or memes — or, worse still, corporate self-congratulatory #SorryNotSorry messaging — will create costly misfires in your remediation strategy that will set back organisational recovery. You will essentially create a crisis within your crisis and risk scuttling the ship.

> 🐦 **Tweet this**
> Crisis content must provide information of value to your audience #SMROE

You can't sell an apology alongside success — it's disingenuous. So leave the 'our track record' and 'our high standards' out of your messaging while navigating through crisis.

3. Torpedoed: your adversaries will use your crisis to their advantage

Nothing screams *abandon ship* louder on social media than an organisation in crisis. Your customers will jump ship to the nearest competitor, your share market hiccup will have investors donning their lifejackets and even your staff will be sizing up the lifeboats ready for a quick exit.

While the world tweets and posts about you (and at you), your competitors and adversaries will be rubbing their hands together with glee and figuring out the best way to capitalise on your fall from grace.

Savvy brands with agency backing will quickly come up with newsjacking ad campaigns. While you can expect direct competitors to join the chorus, you might also find some left-field players entering the fray in a savvy way.

> 🐦 **Tweet this**
> Savvy brands with agency backing will quickly come up with newsjacking ad campaigns #SMROE

IKEA, for example, is fabulous at newsjacking current affairs. Within hours of then Australian Prime Minister Kevin Rudd getting ousted by his own cabinet, IKEA were splashing figure B on- and offline.

Figure B: IKEA is expert at newsjacking

Source: © Inter IKEA Systems B.V.

Of course, poking this kind of fun at your own organisation isn't an option, but don't be surprised by the different ways in which your crisis is leveraged by enterprising newsjackers.

Followship

Do you know when to lead and when to follow?

While we build leaders and promote leadership skills in the corporate and government sectors like commodities, the military have recognised followship as an essential element of teamwork for decades.

Followship is a skill that challenges most of what crisis communicators are taught, yet it's an essential attribute to possess, not only as a leader, but also for your ability to step from team leader to team player.

Former Royal Australian Air Force pilot and Roulettes aerobatic team leader Steve Baker is building a niche in the area of corporate followship. Having headed up teams in high-stakes leadership environments while flying aerobatics at over 450 km/h while pulling 4.5G at around three metres away from the other aircraft in his formation, he understands how critically important followship is within teams. As noted by Steve:

Followship is not about lacking leadership skills, in fact the truth is quite the opposite. Followship is about using your leadership skills to know when to speak up, when to keep quiet, and how to represent the greater good of the team while protecting the integrity of the team leader.

This analogy applies directly to the way crisis communicators and their teams operate and interact with organisations and executives during a crisis.

A crisis communicator must know:

- when to convey advice
- when to keep their advice to themselves (for example, so as not to undermine their CEO publically)
- when to intervene in the boardroom (that is, to 'pick their battles') and
- when to represent the views of the collective.

An integral part of your job as a crisis communicator is to protect and maintain the reputation and leadership ability of your talking head. By all means, be frank and fearless with your advice — just do it privately.

Team systems

No doubt you will be familiar with the term *teamwork*. Who isn't? It's a buzzword that is now several decades old. From a crisis communications perspective, in the social era it's a term that no longer serves us well.

It's time for a rethink.

With technology outpacing our every move and often influencing our decision making, it astounds me that most people still have a hive mentality geared to fit the corporate mould.

In the social era, the construct of traditional 'teamwork' is akin to trying to stick a hashtag in a bowl of alphabet soup. Yes, they are often seen at the same parties, but a hashtag still isn't a letter of the alphabet.

In a crisis communications context (at the very least), forget about teamwork. Welcome to the world of *team systems*.

I first came across this term in Horst M. Rechelbacher's book *Alivelihood: The Art of Sustainable Success*. The idea of team systems, it occurred to me, was a far more accurate and holistic way of approaching working with teams during a social media crisis.

From the outset, rather than looking at the individual teams of an organisation that come together to make it whole, think instead of all those individual teams coming together with a shared vision to create systems of productivity. They aren't separate teams coming together individually; they are teams coming together to build a bigger, better team.

Alone, each team can only achieve so much; but together they form a powerful system that can really make a positive difference to any project they collaborate on — including crisis communications.

Crisis tends to trigger a fight-or-flight response — that is, a determination to stay and fight or an overwhelming desire to flee.

Evidence of the fight-or-flight response is abundant on social media. Some organisations on the firing line go on the defensive and make things worse; others flee the scene of social disaster, creating an information vacuum in their wake.

When the collective 'we' becomes 'me' in an organisational social media crisis, everyone looks to their own survival by moving instinctively toward a fight-or-flight response. Looking after yourself first becomes the priority, and each individual's ability and inclination to help others diminishes.

These outcomes are not particularly helpful for crisis communicators. Which is why building team systems is essential. This is something that the military have long recognised, and because of the high-stakes nature of their work, they train their people specifically to put the collective before the individual during time of crisis.

Crisis communicators should take the same approach. Social media is by definition a social endeavour that both leverages the human desire to 'be part of something' and at the same time influences hive-like behaviours and groupthink.

We know that teams who have not prepared for adversity together 'de-bond' quickly, so as part of your social media crisis communications plan and war game scenarios of social media anarchy. Develop team resilience, confidence and skill by nurturing them in a safe environment *before* you need the team to deliver on those skills.

What happens when the team is the cause of the crisis?

With organisations largely responsible for their own social media crises, dealing with an internal team (or individual) that is the cause of the crisis is a tricky task for crisis communicators.

Setting aside the appropriateness of taking the individual cause out of the situation (as, for instance, in the case of #HasJustineLandedYet), the way to manage team systems during internal crisis is by reinforcing organisational vision.

Acknowledge the natural feelings of resentment and hostility toward the cause of the crisis and give people an appropriate and constructive environment to share that frustration. That could take the form of an intranet group or face-to-face interaction with senior management or a professional mediator. This needs to be timed either to urgently fix team system de-bonding with a view to moving them forward or to be conducted as a debrief *after* the crisis is resolved.

In social media crisis communications, the organisation depends on the success of the individuals within it to recover and move on quickly, so include these elements in your war gaming. But be sure you have more scenarios geared toward an internal focus for this to have effect.

A team system's immunity to internal crises is built not around apathy toward risk but on the acceptance that being on social media presents an accepted level of (and mitigated) risk and the belief that teams can overcome organisational and personal diversity.

It is essential to remind your team systems that collaboration trumps a siloed approach to managing risk. Which makes the post-crisis debrief critically important for internal crises.

A lessons learned approach needs to be taken not only to ensure a repeat crisis doesn't arise, but also to reinforce organisational policies, values and standards of behaviour.

> 🐦 **Tweet this**
> It is essential to remind your team systems that collaboration trumps a siloed approach to managing risk #SMROE

Communication

You probably think this subheading is redundant: in a book about crisis communications, the author is about to tell me what communications means?

Correct.

Because what usually happens during a crisis, whether it's being played out in the newspapers or spreading through social media, is that crisis communicators are so busy communicating with the CEO, the General, the Minister, the media and organisational stakeholders, that they forget to communicate with their own people.

In fact, the easiest people to shut out are your own team members, because more often than not they are the only ones *not* trying to get a piece of you in the whirlpool of 'what next?', 'where are we at?' and 'what should I do?'

How are you going to ensure their need for up-to-date, timely information is met? You may not be able to give them face time; you may not even be in the same building, state or country! But you need to make it work.

Here are ideas garnered from my time running strategic communications teams in crisis and high-tempo environments.

TIPS ON RUNNING CRISIS COMMUNICATIONS TEAMS

Schedule time

Unless you are in dire circumstances, dedicate five or ten minutes every morning and afternoon to your team in which they can raise issues and ask questions. This time should be completely directed by *them* and their needs. The rest of the world will keep spinning while you ignore your emails and let the phone ring. Scheduled time need not be face time: this can be accomplished just as effectively via Skype or telephone.

Establish an information triage

I found group mailboxes particularly useful for this. I could see what was flying back and forth in cyberspace (as could anyone else to whom I gave permission, which reduced the volume of questions I received). Also, I could use different coloured flags to assign tasks to particular team members and/or rank flag colours in order of urgency. If you don't have a group mailbox,

(continued)

TIPS ON RUNNING CRISIS COMMUNICATIONS TEAMS *(cont'd)*

email headers with cues such as [URGENT] or [IN SLOWER TIME] work just as well to help filter tasks.

Take a break

Make sure your team members get plenty of breaks, and by that I mean they leave the office for 30 minutes for lunch or at least step away for some down time. Insist on it. Taking breaks is critically important for maintaining their endurance, focus and clarity. There is nothing like a short walk and fresh air to clear the mind and rejuvenate the senses. Don't forget this applies to you as well.

Feed them

If you know you and your team are going to be captive in your office for a long time, call in the caterers or cater yourself. I did this each and every Senate estimates hearing I ran communications for. There are three reasons for this:

- It's one less decision anyone has to make that day. Think anything from healthy snacks to ordering in pizza, jellybeans and drinks. I was known for turning up on busy mornings with large batches of intricately decorated cupcakes, and ice cream on hand. I may or may not have started a trend by installing a coffee machine in the office – BYO pods! It's the little things that matter when running teams in crisis mode, and people genuinely appreciate thoughtful leaders.

- Catering also offers a hidden bonus: it encourages decision makers to step into *your* space. Everyone loves a good lolly jar and while your CEO or General satisfies a sugar fix in the late afternoon you get five minutes of their undivided attention. Win-win!

- People get hungry! Cafeterias close and vending machine food gets tiresome. Giving your staff a variety of healthy and junk options to eat on the go is much better than losing them for two hours while they find the nearest foodstore that's still open.

Brief and debrief

Briefing them formally in a messaging send-and-receive style is a great way to ensure key people are getting the same advice at the same time. You can do this in person, via video or phone link, or a combination of both. Conversely, after the crisis has dissipated it's just as important to provide event closure and debrief those same stakeholders.

While you should make a short time available for questions, your aim in both situations should be to ensure the information you have provided has been received accurately and everyone understands the current and future state of play.

There is no rule on how many briefs or debriefs you may need to conduct. Let the situation guide you in determining how often people need information and feedback, and what is the best way of delivering those communications to them.

Endurance

Social media doesn't afford much respite during organisational crises, which are rarely short affairs, tending to live on in Google's cache and among the #PRFail recaps for some time to come.

This should tell you two things from a planning perspective:

1   You need to train for the race of the crisis.

2   Win or lose, you need to train for the aftermath of the race.

Organisations, and the people in them, have varying degrees of natural resilience and endurance. It's natural for people to feel a range of emotions in response to workplace stressors, and taking account of this should be part of your social media crisis communications strategy.

For the crisis communicator, the following are early-warning indicators of the state of risk around an organisation's endurance levels.

Recent crises

If your organisation has suffered a string of crises (not all need have been social media related), this can have a profound impact on both the morale of the workforce and the ability of the organisation to support its staff.

Just as workers at the coalface experience fatigue, so too can managers and executives who have been working in a constant state of crisis over long periods of time.

It is essential that the wellbeing, both physical and emotional, of the entire organisation is factored into your social media crisis communications plan. Consider these questions:

- What services do you have available to support the organisation in times of prolonged crisis?

- How can you best activate them in line with your crisis communications plan?

- What signs should managers and supervisors look out for in their teams? And who is looking out for them?

Organisational trauma

If your organisation works in a life-and-death situational environment — such as in the military or law enforcement, or your crisis is the result of a life-threatening or fatal workplace incident — this can create significant distress in the workforce. It can also trigger distress among your social media audience.

Again, the need for external professional help to guide the organisation and its people through this time should not be underestimated. The welfare of those within the organisation and, if the crisis is public, of your social media audience becomes paramount.

You might be thinking, how could I possibly support the strangers that follow me on social media? The answer is quite simple: you listen. You give them the space and a supportive environment and ensure they know where they can find assistance if they need it (through services such as Lifeline[5] and Beyond Blue[6] and other public resources).

These preparations will contribute greatly to an organisation's ability to run the long race during times of crises. So make sure your crisis communications team, and the organisation as a whole, know where to seek assistance when certain events in your risk register occur. Employee support should be a high priority during critical crises, particularly when trauma has occurred.

Organisations need to afford their workforces the time and space to heal from significant trauma just as your social media audience needs time to return to a business-as-usual routine on social media.

From a social media perspective, sharing the crisis can be cathartic. Where circumstances allow, and the timing is right, sharing stories gives people the opportunity to support one another. Just because your social media audience lives in the world behind your screen doesn't mean they are any less human than you.

People who belong to strong social network communities, who have strong brand and organisational affinity, share in each success and loss in the same way as any member of your workforce. Embrace your social circle during these times of crisis if appropriate. Let the H2H (human to human) facet of social networking do what it does best — engage.

After the flood

It might have finished raining, but it can take a while before the floodwaters recede and it's safe to stand on soggy land again. After an organisational crisis, you cannot simply about-face and change your Facebook posts from disaster mode to 'please buy our stuff' again. You are still not at the controls of your ark at this point — your audience is. It's their cues you must read astutely before unloading your ark and packing away the life-vests.

---

5. https://www.lifeline.org.au
6. http://www.beyondblue.org.au

This can be a hard call to make. Transitioning back into business can be a slow process, and it can have bottom-line impacts. But would you prefer to be cautious and considered in your crisis recovery, or to face a backlash from your social media community for attempting to lure them back into sales before they have forgiven you your social media sins or been given time to move on from tragedy?

One organisation that has repeatedly courted controversy by angering their customers one day and attempting to win them over quite shamelessly the next is Australia's iconic airline Qantas, the flying kangaroo.

After their CEO grounded the fleet because of disagreements over industrial action, stranding some 80 000 passengers around the world, the airline's marketing and communications department decided to push through the crisis and attempt to lure their audience back into business-as-usual mode by running the #QantasLuxury competition (see figure C).

Figure C: the beginning of Qantas' #QantasLuxury competition

Qantas Airways @QantasAirways
To enter tell us 'What is your dream luxury inflight experience?
(Be creative!) Answer must include #QantasLuxury.
TCs qantas.com.au/travel/airline …
11:34 AM - 22 Nov 2011

Their social media audience smelled a turkey of a reward[7] (who in all seriousness thinks a set of business-class pajamas makes a good competition prize?). The outrage over the airline's previous bungled grounding the fleet was still fresh in customers' minds. The result, of course, was another social media crisis (see figure D).

---

7. http://www.changefactory.com.au/our-thinking/articles/recognising-a-turkey-of-a-reward

Figure D: another social media crisis

($) Stephen Dann @stephendann 🐦
Flights that leave on schedule because Management doesn't arbitrarily shut down the airline #QantasLuxury
11:42 AM - 22 Nov 2011

Andrew Tan @ndrew10 🐦
RT @kiwi_kali: **#qantasLuxury** somewhere in Qantas HQ a middle aged manager is yelling at a Gen Y social media "expert" to make it stop. / LOL
05:49 PM - 21 Nov 2011

Gordy @GordyPls 🐦
Please familiarise yourself with your career in social media, remembering it could be behind you. #QantasLuxury
12:58 PM - 22 Nov 2011

Fake Alan Joyce @AlanJoyceCEO 🐦
Thanks to the #QantasLuxury stunt, I can see smoke coming out of Tweetdeck on the social media team's computer from my desk. 5 floors away.
12:38 PM - 22 Nov 2011

And Qantas' response (see figure E)?

Figure E: how Qantas responded

Qantas Airways @QantasAirways 🐦
At this rate our #QantasLuxury competition is going to take years to judge.
3:43 PM - 22 Nov 2011

Humour in the face of outrage. Not a wise response.

By misreading audience sentiment and carrying on as if nothing had happened, Qantas disrespected the very community that keeps it flying. It didn't listen to its social community and its pushback into sales and silly competitions was immediately judged as a diversionary tactic.

The lesson: let your audience's sentiment—that is, how well they have moved past your crisis—guide you in timing your return to business as usual.

Plan for a staged return to normal social media communications, but allow some breathing room as you bring your audience back with soft content and human interest stories. Use this intermediate phase as a guide to reassess your speed of return to normal social communications. If you meet resistance, ease back. If you experience wide support, move forward.

Don't hide the elephant in the room. Embrace your crisis and your apology, and demonstrate your resolve to make things right.

Actions speak louder than words, and this is never truer than on social media.

#PayItForward

Putting into words what I'd usually express with a giant hug is harder than writing a book! The people mentioned here are all extraordinary, kindred spirits and I'm incredibly blessed to have them in my life.

If it takes 'a village to raise a child', then I can say with absolute certainty, it takes a 'village of support'—comprising of a small on and offline army—to write a book.

To @LucyRaymond and the team at @WileyBizAus—what a journey. Thank you for believing in me and my story, and for guiding me on this adventure that is being an author.

To my folks Milan and Marija, who instilled in me from an early age the belief that I could achieve anything I put my mind to. Thanks for giving me the greatest gift of all—free, creative thought.

To my brother Dan and sister Kat: when did we all grow up?

To my industrious brother—from whom I learned what hardcover books were *really* useful for when Mum reached for the wooden spoon—thanks for being your laid back, easy going self.

To my clever sister—who I'll credit with giving me at a young age my first lessons in PSYOP as I marveled at your ability to always make our folks think 'it was someone else's fault'—thanks for being your witty, intelligent self.

To my Twitter sister, @pod_legal aka Karan White—when I asked the twitterverse who my 800th tweep would be, it sent me you! Your unwavering support and positivity is an incredible gift, thank you for sharing it with me.

To @SteveVallas at my local, South Melbourne's @TheHoneyBar, and his wife Jasmin—thanks for the conversations, the cocktails, the endless encouragement and your wise words of wisdom. Cheers to real conversations about real life.

To my BrisVegas bestie Kendall Barry — thanks for being such an incredible source of encouragement, inspiration and support.

To @TrevorYoung aka the @PRWarrior — thank you for being such an amazing advocate, trusted adviser, supporter and friend.

To Steve Baker aka @RouletteLeader — your friendship has both inspired and healed me. Thanks for being there, always.

To my @InfoOpsHQ business partner @DavidBaileyMBE — thanks for reaching out, for believing in me and for joining me on this vital mission.

To my digital doppelganger @JoshRowe #GoTiges #MissChu — thanks for your endless encouragement and positivity.

To my Defence family:

@TheKateSpace aka Kate Davis — my amazing friend who has been so incredibly generous in her ongoing support and encouragement — thank you Katey-D!

To Dougie McGuire — thanks for the laughs and honest reflections on situations that are just fubar'ed. Don't ever change.

To Helen Ward — thanks for your unwavering support and friendship and for being an incredible mentor during challenging times.

To Claire Reynolds from Melbourne to Ispwich to Seoul — my inspiring mentor — thanks for letting me ride shotgun on some of your amazing adventures.

To my Customs and Border Protection family: Roula Butterworth, Alen-Igor Radonjic, Glenn Ware, Rish Saraw (and his wife Seema) thanks for your enduring friendship and for sharing some of the most incredible unpublishable professional experiences with me.

To my school pals Alice and Jason Osborne — thanks for the moniker 'Miss Cole'. It's been a delight reconnecting with you and your gorgeous family. Your endless encouragement and support has been such a blessing.

To Jamie White aka @PodLegal — thank you for your legal expertise, guidance and enduring support of my adventures.

To @DionneLew aka The Social Executive—thanks for your enthusiasm and endless support. You are an inspiration.

To @JordanaOz aka Jordana Borensztajn—my #twinz—thanks for the LOLs the brunches, the endless encouragement and for being an awesome friend.

To @YvonneAdele—thanks for the friendship, the flowers, the beach/tan walks and for opening up your world to another crazy adventurer. You rock.

To 'Bob', Mel Macdougall and Brendan Saritschniy—who have been with me the longest on this wild ride—once a freelancer always a freelancer.

To @MottsMelb aka @CXpert—thanks for helping me crowdsource an AFL team to follow, #GoTiges, and for being one of my earliest tweeps, and my long-time twitter conversationalist. Batman, you're the best!

To @Ric_Cole and @MHWenham—thanks for your constant support and inspiration from the other side of this amazing world.

To the NATO team at ACT's Innovation Hub, @SergeDDS @Innov8Hub—thanks for inviting me on one of the best professional adventures a blogger could dream of #SM4NATO

To the @IABCVIC Board of 2012-14—thank you for your endless support and encouragement.

To Kevin Dwyer and the team at Melbourne's @ChangeFactory—thanks for taking a punt on me early on in my consultancy career, and for penning one of my favourite mantras: 'Succeed Despite, Don't Fail Because.'

Thank you, everyone.

Index

Connect
with WILEY ▶▶▶

WILEY

Browse and purchase the full range of Wiley publications on our official website.

www.wiley.com

Check out the Wiley blog for news, articles and information from Wiley and our authors.

www.wileybizaus.com

Join the conversation on Twitter and keep up to date on the latest news and events in business.

@WileyBizAus

Sign up for Wiley newsletters to learn about our latest publications, upcoming events and conferences, and discounts available to our customers.

www.wiley.com/email

Wiley titles are also produced in e-book formats. Available from all good retailers.

WILEY

Learn more with practical advice from our experts

Ignite
Gabrielle Dolan

Microdomination
Trevor Young

The Social Executive
Dionne Kasian-Lew

The Great Fragmentation
Steve Sammartino

Above the Line
Michael Henderson

Humanise
Anthony Howard

On Purpose
Karen James

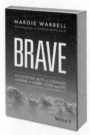

Brave
Margie Warrell

Conscious Marketing
Carolyn Tate

Available in print and e-book formats

WILEY